KUSMINDER CHAHA

SUPPORTING VICTIMS OF HATE CRIME

A practitioner guide

POLICY PRESS SHORTS POLICY & PRACTICE

First published in Great Britain in 2017 by

Policy Press
University of Bristol
1-9 Old Park Hill
Bristol
BS2 8BB
UK
+44 (0)117 954 5940
pp-info@bristol.ac.uk
www.policypress.co.uk

North America office:
Policy Press
c/o The University of Chicago Press
1427 East 60th Street
Chicago, IL 60637, USA
t: +1 773 702 7700
f: +1 773 702 9756
sales@press.uchicago.edu
www.press.uchicago.edu

British Library Cataloguing in Publication Data
A catalogue record for this book is available from the British Library.

Library of Congress Cataloging-in-Publication Data
A catalog record for this book has been requested.

ISBN 978-1-4473-2972-5 (paperback)
ISBN 978-1-4473-2974-9 (ePub)
ISBN 978-1-4473-2975-6 (Mobi)
ISBN 978-1-4473-2973-2 (ePdf)

Cover design by Policy Press
Front cover: image kindly supplied by istock

This book is dedicated in
memory of my friend,
Professor Bogusia Temple
(1954–2016)

Contents

Acknowledgments

I would like to thank Professor Harris Beider for his day-to-day support and encouragement, and Professor Corinne May-Chahal for providing expertise in Chapter Two.

Author biography

Kusminder Chahal is a Research Associate at the Centre for Trust, Peace and Social Relations, Coventry University, UK.

1

HATE CRIME BASICS

Hate crime casework and support involves providing emotional support, practical assistance and advice to people and groups who have reported, accessed or been referred to a support service or professional (eg a hate crime practitioner, police officer, housing officer, social worker or teacher). Guidance on providing effective casework support to hate crime victims is limited and this guide offers information, advice and frameworks for a busy practitioner to develop their working practices with clients.

The first two chapters of the book focus on current hate crime knowledge, including the increase in hate crime in the digital world. Chapters Three and Four provide an insight into current rights-based frameworks for victim support, as well as the needs of and approach to working with hate crime victims. Chapters Five and Six introduce the role of the caseworker working with hate crime victims, and the underpinning principles and approaches to support. Chapters Seven and Eight explore the interpersonal skills required to communicate with clients and the minimum that needs to be considered in the process of fact finding with the client. Chapter Nine recognises the self-care needs of caseworkers themselves.

What is hate crime casework support?

Both European Union (EU) and UK policy has, in recent years, shifted to recognising the needs of hate crime victims and the services and responsibilities that reporting agencies (particularly within the criminal justice system) have. The recent EU directive establishing minimum standards on the rights, support and protection of victims of crime calls on member states to establish specialised victim support services, either as an integrated part of or in addition to generic victim support services (European Commission, 2012). However, independent hate crime support services and dedicated practitioners are unevenly distributed, although they do provide an important service for victims (Chahal, 2003; Jalota, 2004). Hate crime practitioners work in a variety of settings, including non-government organisations (NGOs) and the public and private sector, to provide support, advice and assistance to victims.

There are five key identified tasks that are central to effective hate crime casework support:

- believing and offering help;
- reducing the immediate impact of the violence;
- aiming to resolve the complaint through an agreed intervention or series of interventions;
- client empowerment; and
- developing professional practice (Chahal, 2008; Kees et al, 2016).

The police are the primary agency that hate crimes are reported to and play the most prominent role in referring victims to access support services (Victim Support Europe, 2013). However, not all individuals and groups feel comfortable or secure in approaching them. This is particularly so where the police are perceived as part of the problem and are not trusted by people, for example, by those who have escaped repressive regimes and are seeking asylum or by those who lack confidence that the police (or other relevant agencies) will recognise and respond to the hate crime experience. Hate crime casework and support responds to the need that victims are likely to require a supportive mechanism that believes, builds confidence and empowers people whose lives are often shattered to move forward. Box 1.1 lists the direct and indirect support that many hate crime service providers (and generic victim support services) offer to their clients.

Box 1:1: Direct and indirect victim support

Direct victim support	**Indirect victim support**
Practical support	Monitoring hate crime
Emotional support	Research
Advocacy	Media work
Counselling and psychological advice	Promoting victims' rights
Empowerment	Policy work
Medical advice	Report writing
Financial assistance	Training
Referrals	Community work
Court/witness assistance	Education
Court-based work	Increasing awareness
Legal advice/support	Campaigning
Mediation	
Supporting victims of far-right violence	

Defining hate crime

Hate crimes and incidents are motivated by prejudice, hostility and intolerance and are targeted at individuals because of their perceived affiliation with a group that shares a particular characteristic (ODIHR, 2009). The Home Office observes that hate crime has a 'harmful effect on its victims, as it seeks to attack an intrinsic part of who they are perceived to be' (Home Office, 2016: 9) and, in this sense, is 'pernicious' (Home Office, 2016: 12) because it transmits a message not just to the victim, but to the wider community, that their behaviour, cultural norms or presence will not be tolerated (Garland and Chakraborti, 2012: 3).

Therefore, the symbolic nature of hate crime means that it acts as a message crime: that it could lead to further violence if the victim continues with conduct that the perpetrator views as unacceptable (Garland and Chakraborti, 2012: 3). It is recognised that hate itself may only form a small part of the commission of hate crime. Bias and prejudice may be the primary motivators and, as such, in the US, for example, 'bias crime' is often used interchangeably with 'hate crime' (Garland and Chakraborti, 2012).

What makes a crime a hate crime?

Hate crime describes acts that are committed with a bias motive, and the types of criminal acts are written in law. Hate itself is not legally defined. It is the motivation of bias, prejudice and hostility that constitutes the enhancement to a hate crime. Hate crime comprises two elements: an act that constitutes an offence under criminal law; and in committing the crime, the perpetrator acts on the basis of prejudice or bias (ODIHR, 2009: 15). This involves a perpetrator deliberately and consciously choosing and targeting a victim because of a real or perceived protected characteristic. The crime could also be victimless in that a property is targeted (eg a religious building) that is associated with or perceived to be associated with a particular social group or characteristic.

Currently, in the UK, there are five centrally monitored strands (protected characteristics) of hate crime that have legal protection:

- disability;
- race or ethnicity;
- religion or beliefs;
- sexual orientation; and
- transgender identity.

Hate crime is seen as having harmful effects on its victims, on communities, and impacts on social cohesion within society. As such, penalty enhancements are considered or applied if a crime can be shown to have been targeted at a person motivated by hostility or prejudice based on the five legally defined 'monitored strands'. While hate crime is not a specific offence in UK criminal law, a hate crime caseworker can draw on a range of existing offences that are committed against the person, which includes threats, harassment, physical assault and damage to property. There are further offences of incitement to violence or hatred that may be directed not at individuals, but at groups or indirectly threaten individuals (see Appendix 1 for current legislation).

Practice-based definitions

The inquiry into the murder of Stephen Lawrence (Macpherson, 1999) demonstrated that black and minority ethnic people in the UK are targeted for 'everyday' and politically organised racist violence and this enduring experience influences how they think, feel and act (Bowling and Phillips, 2003). The Macpherson Inquiry was instrumental in shifting the power balance in operational definitions of racist hate incidents, putting a focus on the victim's perception:

> *A racist incident is any incident which is perceived to be racist by the victim or any other person.* (Macpherson, 1999: 328)

The perception of the victim rather than an investigating officer is important to the incident being recorded as a racist incident. As such, the definition shifted from dismissing the concerns and experiences of victims, to their version of events being accepted until an investigation found otherwise. This foregrounded the realities of racist violence and the numbers of racist crimes recorded subsequently increased year on year. However, the definition takes a universal approach to racist incidents – anyone can be a victim – and this was further embedded in how the Lawrence Inquiry operationalised racism as 'conduct or words or practices which advantage or disadvantage people because of their colour, culture or ethnic origin' (Macpherson, 1999: 321).

The umbrella term 'hate crime' covers a range of 'monitored strands' and has operational definitions that also focus on the perception of the victim and a third party, characterising 'hate' as demonstrations of hostility, prejudice, ill will or malice. In 2007, the Crown Prosecution Service (CPS), police and criminal justice agencies across England and

Wales adopted a broad operational definition of hate crime that is used primarily for recording purposes:

> *A hate crime is any criminal offence which is perceived by the victim or any other person, to be motivated by hostility or prejudice towards someone based on a personal characteristic.* (Corcoran et al, 2015: 2)

In England, Wales and Northern Ireland, a perpetrator-focused definition for hate crime and incidents is:

> *any crime or incident where the perpetrator's hostility or prejudice against an identifiable group of people is a factor in determining who is victimised.* (College of Policing, 2014: 3)

In Scotland, hate crime is defined as:

> *a crime perceived as being motivated by malice or ill will towards a particular social group on the basis of their actual or presumed sexual orientation, transgender identity, disability, race or religion.* (see: www.scotland.police.uk)

Contesting hate crime categories

Garland and Chakraborti (2012: 12) observe that 'Hate crime is an inherently problematic concept. Over the few decades of its existence it has proved controversial and divisive, with its precise meaning elusive and its parameters vague'. There is, indeed, little consensus on what constitutes a 'hate crime', why and how, although it is described and recognised as a global phenomenon (Winterdyk and Antonopoulos, 2008; Iganski and Levin, 2015). Hate crime has been categorised as 'a somewhat slippery notion' (Chakraborti and Garland, 2009: 7). The contested nature of hate crime and the social groups who are excluded from being identified as its potential targets, and therefore monitored and afforded legal protection, is illustrated by the findings of consultation undertaken by the College of Policing: 'The five strands of monitored hate crime *are the minimum categories* that police officers and staff are expected to record.... During consultation to agree the monitored strands, a further 21 different groups were identified for consideration' (College of Policing, 2014: 7, emphasis added).

Hate crime, as a 'slippery notion', may present problems for practitioners. Victims of crime who are targeted because of a perceived characteristic but not a 'monitored strand' may feel excluded from recognition as hate crime victims and from appropriate support services. However, hate crime is an elastic concept. The College of Policing (2014: 7) has advised that different social groups may be included locally as hate crime victims if there is a concern (see Box 1.2). This has the potential to increase access to and demands on victim support services.

Box 1.2: Claiming hate victimisation status

In the summer of 2007, Sophie Lancaster and Robert Maltby were attacked by a gang of teenagers in a park in Bacup, Lancashire, whom they had earlier befriended. Robert was attacked first, being punched and kicked, and when on the ground, he was kicked to the head and body and at least one attacker stamped on his head. Sophie attempted to help Robert and was calling for help and shouting at the attackers to leave him alone. She, too, was attacked, which involved kicking and stamping, and both were left unconscious. A witness who rang the emergency services, herself crying hysterically throughout the call, identified Sophie and Robert as 'moshers' (another term for goths), stating: 'this mosher's just been banged up because he's a mosher' (Garland, 2010). Both were rushed to hospital and Sophie died from her injuries 14 days later. At the trial that followed, the prosecution said that Sophie and Robert had been 'singled out ... because they dressed differently', and in passing sentence, the judge identified the assault as 'a hate crime against these completely harmless people who were targeted because their appearance was different' (Hodkinson, 2008).

The Observer (Hodkinson, 2008) reported a year later that Bacup is 'isolated from major towns and cities' and 'sits in a steep-sided valley. Much of its infrastructure is derelict ... several shops are empty ... on the hillsides are several notorious estates'. The area is identified as a 'shit-hole' and has an identifiable absence of black and minority ethnic people, who 'get fired-bombed out of their houses and given a whack with a baseball bat to make sure they get the message'.

A campaign to highlight the issue of prejudice and hatred faced by alternative cultures and goths and to recognise this locally as a hate crime was launched by Sophie Lancaster's family. This led to Greater Manchester Police (GMP) being the first police authority to record and monitor hate crimes and incidents against people from alternative subcultures in April 2013. However, this is not a government-recognised monitored strand (characteristic), nor does it have any legal status or protection.

The murder of Sophie Lancaster and the subsequent recognition by some police authorities of alternative subcultures as potential targets of hate victimisation raise the issue of what actually constitutes a hate crime (Garland, 2010). This is important to recognise from a practitioner perspective because it means that the conceptual category of 'hate crime' is not fixed, but fluid, dynamic and politically changeable depending on context, events, the power of victims' lobbying and social movements. Indeed, the working definitions of hate crime are so broad and inclusive that 'a victim does not have to be a member of the group in fact, anyone could be a victim of hate crime' (College of Policing, 2014: 3). 'Hate crime' is a porous organising category that different social groups will utilise, campaign on and activate to achieve victim status and recognition. As such, what we know now as the official measurable extent of hate crime will change as the boundaries of what is classified as a hate crime continue to be extended.

Extent of hate crime

There are two main official sources for the extent of hate crime offences in England and Wales: the Crime Survey for England and Wales (CSEW)[1] and the annual police-recorded crime data. In Northern

Ireland the Police Service of Northern Ireland (PSNI) provides yearly figures on both hate motivated incidents and crimes. In Scotland, the Procurator Fiscal provides details of yearly reported hate crime charges. A third source comes in the way of local or national inquiries and prevalence surveys with specific social groups (eg Victim Support, 2006; EHRC, 2011; Guasp et al, 2013; Chakraborti and Hardy, 2016).

Police-recorded crime

In 2015/16, there were 62,518 hate crimes recorded across the five monitored strands by the police in England and Wales. This was an increase of 19% on the previous recording year and an increase in all of the five monitored strands (Corcoran and Smith, 2016: 4). Of the 62,518 hate crimes in England and Wales:

- 49,419 (79%) were race hate crimes;
- 7,194 (12%) were sexual orientation hate crimes;
- 4,400 (7%) were religious hate crimes;
- 3,629 (6%) were disability hate crimes; and
- 858 (1%) were transgender hate crimes.

In 2015/16, the Police Service of Northern Ireland (2016) recorded 3,108 incidents, including sectarian incidents, with a hate motivation:

- 1,352 (44%) were sectarian incidents;
- 1,221 (39%) were racist incidents;
- 343 (11%) were homophobic incidents;
- 134 (4%) were disability incidents;
- 39 (1%) were faith/religion incidents; and
- 19 (1%) were transphobic incidents.

In Scotland, there were a total of 5,831 hate crime charges reported in 2015/16 (Crown Office and Procurator Fiscal Service, 2016):

- 3,712 (63%) were race crimes;
- 1,020 (17.5%) were sexual orientation crimes;
- 581 (10%) were religious crimes;
- 201 (4%) were disability crimes;
- 287 (5%) were offensive behaviour at football matches; and
- 30 (0.5%) were transgender identity crimes.

Year on year since 2012/13, hate crime has increased across the monitored strands in England and Wales. In Northern Ireland, hate crimes decreased across all the hate incident types except homophobic incidents. In Scotland, there was an increase in all categories of hate crime reporting compared to the previous year except in race crimes which saw the lowest number of reported hate crimes since 2003/04. Generally, reporting increases would suggest that hate crime services will be seeing a growth in referrals and demand for support.

Crime Survey for England and Wales

Based on combined data from the years 2012/13 to 2014/15, the Crime Survey for England and Wales (CSEW) (Corcoran et al, 2015: 1) found that:

- there were 220,000 hate crimes on average per year for the five monitored strands;
- 106,000 hate crime incidents were motivated by race per year (48% of the total); and
- 70,000 hate crime incidents were motivated by disability (32% of the total).

The CSEW highlights: that the extent of hate crime is far greater than official recorded data would suggest; that under-reporting is a major issue particularly with disability hate crime; and that there is a discrepancy between police-recorded and reported hate crime figures.

Types of hate crime

Verbal abuse and harassment are by far the most common hate experience (Chahal and Julienne, 1999; Victim Support, 2006; Chakraborti et al, 2014), often described by victims as everyday occurrences. In a recent study, 87% of all hate crime victims had suffered verbal abuse (Chakraborti et al, 2014). Verbal abuse is also the least likely incident to be reported to the police or another relevant organisation (Chakraborti and Hardy, 2016). Chakraborti et al (2014: 18) found that disabled respondents reported the largest numbers of everyday experiences of hate crime: 92% experienced harassment, 90% verbal abuse, 50% violent crime and 22% sexual violence.

Surveys since the 1980s on hate crime and victimisation have identified the types and effects of hate victimisation, which have an enduring familiar theme that has again recently been highlighted:

> Participants' experiences of victimisation were extremely diverse, and included being sent hate mail, or offensive text messages; having the windows of their family car smashed repeatedly; being mimicked and mocked for a speech impediment or physical disability; having eggs thrown at their house or faeces pushed through their letter box; being befriended and then exploited, humiliated or robbed; and being intimidated and threatened at work, in the street, in pubs, clubs and restaurants and at home. (Chakraborti et al, 2014: 17)

The CSEW found that 49% of hate crime incidents involved violence, including 19% involving criminal damage, compared with only 19% of overall crime involving violence (Corcoran et al, 2015: 15). The CSEW found that 59% of offences flagged as hate crimes by the police were primarily public order offences, compared with 4% for overall crime. Of hate crime public order offences, 98% were public fear, alarm or distress, 30% were violence against the person and 7% were criminal damage/arson (Corcoran et al, 2015: 8). Hate crime victims are more likely to suffer violent attacks and harassment than overall crime victims.

The effects of hate crime

It has long been identified that there are emotional and psychological impacts on hate crime victims (Virdee, 1995; Chahal and Julienne, 1999; Victim Support, 2006). In recent years, as the 'monitored strands' for hate have expanded, national and local surveys, the CSEW, and academic research have begun to highlight the consequences of hate crime on everyday lives and decision-making across the strands (eg Iganski, 2008; EHRC, 2011; Chakraborti et al, 2014).

The question 'Does hate crime hurt more?' is one that has had some attention in the UK since the Stephen Lawrence Inquiry (Macpherson, 1999). Iganski (2001) recognised that there were identifiable impacts on victims but that the effects beyond this initial impact required empirical exploration, not least to identify how services may be able to respond to the needs of victims of hate crime. Iganski (2008) analysed 2002–05 British Crime Survey data and found '*elevated psychological damage to hate victims*' (Walters and Hoyle, 2010: 230, emphasis added) compared to non-hate crime victims.

Research in the US has confirmed that the elevated damage includes long-term post-traumatic stress disorder, fear, anxiety, loss of confidence and depression (Herek et al, 1997; Craig-Henderson and Sloan, 2003; see also Box 1.3). UK-based research on disabled victims of hate crime shows more damaging post-victimisation psychological impacts than for victims of parallel crimes (Iganski and Lagou, 2015). The CSEW (Corcoran et al, 2015: 22) has shown that hate crime victims:

- are more likely than victims of crime overall to say that they were emotionally affected and more likely to be 'very much' affected (36%, compared with 13% of all victims of crime);
- are more likely than victims of crime overall to say that they suffered a loss of confidence or had felt vulnerable after the incident (39%, compared with 17% of all victims of crime); and

- were twice as likely to experience fear, difficulty sleeping, anxiety or panic attacks, or depression compared with all victims of crime.

However, Iganski and Lagou (2015) have also identified that there are variations among victims of racist crime when reporting post-victimisation reactions, suggesting that while hate crimes do hurt more, some hurt more than others. The potential implication on casework practice is that support and responses will need to be tailored specifically to the individual and not a one-size-fits-all approach. There are also identified differences of experience across gender and age in relation to type and frequency, for example, men were more likely than women to have experienced violent hate crime (Chakraborti et al, 2014) and 16–24 year olds were more likely to experience personal hate crime compared with men aged over 75 (Corcoran et al, 2015: 16).

Recording and under-reporting of hate crime

The difference between the police-recorded hate crime figure of 52,465 and an estimated CSEW figure of 106,000 hate incidents that came to the attention of the police means that only an estimated 50% of hate crime experiences were recorded by the police in 2014/15, suggesting significant under-recording. (Corcoran et al, 2015: 18). Reporting outstrips recording by at least two to one. Under-reporting of hate crime is an identified problem for both hate crime victims and overall crime victims. The recent UK government hate crime action plan (Home Office, 2016) has identified a number of social groups who under-report:

- disabled people;
- Muslim women;
- the Charedi community;
- transgender people;
- Gypsy, Traveller and Roma people; and
- new refugees.

Box 1.3: Experiences and reactions to hate victimisation

Experience of hate victimisation

Verbal abuse

Harassment

Bullying

Cyber-hate/bullying

Property crime

Violent crime

Sexual assault/rape

Location of hate victimisation

Public street or park

Outside/near/in someone else's or in the victim's home

In a place of work/study

In the city centre

In or near social setting/location

Public transport

Place of worship

Defence/coping strategies

Retaliate

Avoid certain areas

Reduce risk

Change daily routine

Stop going out

Conceal identity

Use alcohol or drugs

Improve home security

Reporting

Tell family and friends

Post-victimisation indicators

Anger

Anxiety

Crying

Depression

Devalued

Difficulty concentrating

Fear

Insecurity

Worry (financial burden)

Loss of confidence and self-esteem

Panic attacks

Physical ailments

Reduced feelings of safety

Difficulty sleeping

Suicide ideation

Trauma in children

Increased vulnerability

Source: Adapted from Chahal and Julienne (1999), Chakraborti et al (2014) and Iganski (2008).

A number of studies confirm that hate crime under-reporting is extensive. The Gay British Crime Survey (Guasp et al, 2013) found that 75% of those experiencing a hate crime or incident did not report it to the police. Chakraborti et al (2014) found that the majority (56%) of respondents did not report and only 24% said that they had reported their most recent experience of hate crime to the police. This figure was further reduced if the hate crime was based on sexual orientation or alternative dress, appearance and lifestyle (Chakraborti et al, 2014: 66). The survey further found that:

- 16% of victims of verbal abuse reported to the police, which was the largest category of hate victimisation;
- 36% of victims of cyber-bullying reported to the police;
- victims were more likely to report property crime (62%); and
- the primary reason to report was because it was seen as a serious crime.

Victims often decide that a serious crime is a physical attack with injury and/or property damage (Chahal and Julienne, 1999). It is also established that the higher the perceived seriousness of a crime, the greater the chance that it will be reported to the police (Christmann and Wong, 2010). Hence, this may explain the low numbers of reported verbal abuse.

Satisfaction levels with the police

The CSEW found that contact with the police resulted in low satisfaction levels. Only 52% of hate crime victims were very or fairly satisfied with the police's handling of the reported incident, compared with 73% for crime overall, and hate crime victims were more likely to be very dissatisfied (35%) with the police's handling of the matter than overall CSEW crime victims (14%) (Corcoran et al, 2015: 21). The Gay British Crime Survey found that 50% of respondents said that they were dissatisfied with the way in which the police handled the case.

Reporting, non-reporting and satisfaction levels are connected and can lead to a perception that nothing will be done or, indeed, that what the victim has experienced is not an offence (Guasp et al, 2013). Successful prosecutions are crucial to increasing public confidence in the criminal justice system and increasing reporting and satisfaction rates.

Hate crime prosecutions

In 2015/16, the Crown Prosecution Service (CPS) completed 15,442 hate crime prosecutions in England and Wales. This was the highest ever number of prosecutions and included: the highest ever proportion of sentence uplifts in racially and religiously aggravated crimes; the highest ever conviction rate in homophobic and transphobic prosecutions; and a 41% increase in disability hate crime prosecutions compared to 2014/15 (CPS, 2016). Disability hate crime and increasing reporting have been recognised as priorities in recent government hate crime action plans (Home Office, 2016).

Table 1.1, based on complete data from 2015/16, highlights that while improvements have been made in rates of prosecution, there is a large attrition rate across all the hate crime strands, namely, that less than one in four hate crimes reported result in a successful prosecution. This has huge implications for caseworkers and support services:

- How will practitioners respond and manage a victim's disappointment with the investigative process?
- How may that disappointment hamper recovery from the trauma caused by hate violence? and
- How can victim support services increase confidence in public campaigns to encourage communities to report hate crimes?

Table 1.1: Attrition rates from reporting to successful prosecution of hate crime in England and Wales (2015/16)

	Disability	Race	Religion	Sexual orientation	Transgender	Total
Crime Survey for England and Wales estimate	70,000	106,000	38,000	29,000	Unavailable	
No. of hate crimes reported in 2015/16	3,629	49,419	4,400	7,194	858	65,500
No. of crimes prosecuted in 2015/16	941	12,295	737	1,384	85	15,442
Successful outcome in 2015/16	707	10,337	583	1,151	68	12,220
Conviction rate	75.1%	84.1%	79.1%	83.0%	80.0%	83.2%
Attrition rate	80.5%	79.1%	86.7%	84.0%	92.1%	84.5%

Source: Adapted from Home Office (2016).

Summary

This chapter has shown the range of practice-based hate crime definitions, the extent, types and effects of hate crime, and indicators of post-victimisation. Hate crime as a concept is not fixed and practice definitions suggest that everyone can be a victim of hate crime. Hate crime is under-reported, with significant under-reporting of disability hate crime. It is largely the most serious hate crime that is reported and, as such, the support needs of victims presenting at support services may be greater. Chapter Two focuses on the challenges of the digital world and the nature and scope of online hate crime.

Note

[1]   The CSEW is a face-to-face survey in which people resident in households in England and Wales are asked about their experiences of crime in the 12 months prior to the interview.

2
HATE IN A DIGITAL WORLD

The digital world has changed the nature and scope of hate crime. In the UK, 82% of adults (41.8 million) now use the internet almost daily (ONS, 2016), and 98% of children aged 12–15 have internet access, with 5–15 year olds spending an average of 13.7 hours per week online (Ofcom, 2015). The rapid increase in online use, alongside developments in technology, means that hate crime caseworkers and victims live in a digital world. This refers to the way in which the offline and online space converges in everyday life (May-Chahal et al, 2014).

Digital exposure covers much more than mobile phones, laptops and computers; as the move towards the Internet of Things (IoT) progresses (cars, domestic appliances, surveillance and body technologies), the digital world expands. However, beneficial aspects of digitisation, such as connectivity, supporting social relationships and access to new knowledge, have a negative side. This emerging environment has brought a 'startling' and rapid rise in cyber-hate across the world (Citron and Norton, 2011). There is a pressing need to develop processes to support victims of cyber-hate crime, to learn more about how hate crime plays out in on/offline convergent spaces and to discover what can be done about it from a policy and practice perspective. The digital world has changed hate crime in at least three ways:

- people have become much more accessible – information security and the capacity to maintain privacy boundaries, which once may have offered some respite and safety, are harder to maintain when they can be infiltrated by hackers, social media, text and email;

- the reach of people committing hate crimes has extended – people can commit crimes from any part of the world directed at people in the UK; and
- the capacity to commit hate crime has increased – people operate in more extreme ways in online environments, saying and doing things that they would not offline, including threatening and abusive behaviour.

According to 'disinhibition' and 'deindividuation' theory (Zimbardo, 1969; Suler, 2004), when people go online, they appear more able to dissociate from their actions through the ability to remain anonymous and personally invisible, which can result in the loss of a sense of individual responsibility for extreme online behaviours. Such behaviours manifest in things like Twitter mobbing, trolling, cyber-bullying, hate speech, sexting and identity theft (for an example of the trolling of Mary Beard, a prominent British historian and scholar, after her appearance on Question Time, see Box 2.1).

Box 2.1: Trolling: the case of Mary Beard

It all started when Beard appeared as a panellist on the BBC1 programme, filmed in Lincoln. In response to a question about whether the UK could cope with more immigration, she cited a recent report claiming that immigration had actually brought some benefits to the local area – a perfectly reasonable thing to say, or so you might have thought.

However, the next day, commenters on the now-closed Don't Start Me Off website, which encouraged anonymous posters to vent their anger on targets chosen by the administrator, launched a vicious and sustained attack on Beard. The Internet trolls posted dozens of horrifying sexual taunts, in language too offensive to reprint. The level of the abuse was so shocking that even those accustomed to the cut and thrust of online debate were appalled.

In one of the milder examples, Beard was called 'a vile, spiteful excuse for a woman, who eats too much cabbage and has cheese straws for teeth'. Beard's features were even superimposed on an image of female genitalia.

'It was so ghastly it didn't feel personal, or personally critical', Beard says now, with the benefit of considered hindsight. 'It was such generic, violent misogyny. In a way, I didn't feel it was about me.' (Day, 2013)

The nature and extent of hate crime online

Most research to date has sought to identify hate crime issues pertaining to specific characteristics such as race, religion, sexuality, disability and gender (for a review on race, see eg, Daniels, 2013). Recently, social media researchers have begun to take a more generic view. Silva et al (2016) analysed hate speech in a data set comprised of posts collected on Whisper for one year from 6 June 2014 to 6 June 2015 (48.97 million 'whispers') and a 1% random sample of posts on Twitter for the same period (1.6 billion tweets, 512 million of which were in English). The researchers used 'Hatebase' to find key terms – a crowd-sourced database described as 'the world's largest online repository of structured, multilingual, usage-based hate speech' (Silva et al, 2016: 3). Key terms were then categorised and the data was searched for frequencies of occurrence. The highest percentage of hate targets focused on race in both sites; over a third of posts in Whisper and almost half in Twitter (see Table 2.1).

Table 2.1: Distribution of hate speech online

Categories	Examples of hate targets	Twitter (%)	Whisper (%)
Race	'Nigga', black people, white people	48.73	35.81
Behaviour	Insecure people, sensitive people	37.05	19.27
Physical	Obese people, beautiful people	3.38	14.06
Sexual orientation	Gay people, straight people	1.86	9.32
Class	Ghetto people, rich people	1.08	3.63
Gender	Pregnant people, sexist people	0.57	1.96
Ethnicity	Chinese people, Indian people, 'Paki'	0.56	1.89
Disability	'Retard', bipolar people	0.19	0.82
Religion	Religious people, Jewish	0.07	0.41
Other	Drunk people, shallow people	6.50	12.84

Source: Silva et al (2016).

Jacks and Adler (2015) propose a typology containing four different kinds of hate crime perpetrators online:

- *Browsers*: These people may accidentally pick up hate-relevant content online or be deliberately searching for it, but they are characterised as browsers because they do not generally interact with it or act upon the content they find. This content may reinforce already-existing views or socialise people into hate crime and harassment by normalising it.
- *Commentators*: Browsers may also comment on content and generate a 'cycle of action' (Levin, 1999) that pulls others into the online interaction. These people are often part of the 'Twitter mob' described in Box 2.1, responding to posts using hate speech and reinforcing extreme views.
- *Activists*: These people use the internet to extend offline activities. They will initiate posts and mobilise support for their actions and engage with other extremist groups online.

- *Leaders*: Described by Jacks and Adler (2015) as 'the most serious/engaged internet hate user' and the most likely to commit hate crime, leaders originate hate content, hate/extremist websites and initiate planned hate crime activities.

Taking the specific case of Islamophobia, Awan (2014) identified other types of actors in a random sample of 500 tweets from 100 different Twitter users using three hashtags that had 'trended' in 2013 in the UK (#Woolwich, #Muslim and #Islam): 'Accessories', who join in the conversations of others; 'Disseminators', who retweet offensive comments; and 'Impersonators', who retweet offensive comments using fake accounts and profiles. There were also examples of 'reactive' people, who use an incident as a platform to campaign against others, and 'professionals', who have an extensive Twitter following and launch major hate campaigns.

Box 2.2: Word cloud of most frequently used online Islamophobic hate terms

Source: Awan (2014).

Word associations are profoundly offensive (see Box 2.2); in Awan's data, 'Muslim' emerged as most often associated with 'Paedos', a group almost unanimously reviled (for similar findings, see also Tell MAMA, 2014). Along with terms such as 'terrorists', 'pigs' and 'Muslimscum', this speech act association (Asquith, 2010) works to extend highly negative connotations that are quite specific to one religious group.

Impacts of online hate crime

Much of this online hate text could be construed as group-directed or individually targeted 'cyber-harassment', which describes:

> *the intentional infliction of substantial emotional distress accomplished by online speech that is persistent enough to amount to a 'course of conduct' rather than an isolated incident.* (Citron, 2014: 3)

It can involve violent threats that even when directed at a group, can make individuals who claim that identity feel very unsafe and insecure. When targeted at individuals, the impacts can be severe. Drawing on work in other cybercrime sectors (Hasebrink et al, 2009), digital world hate crime can be conceived as having at least three kinds of impact:

- *Content*: People see hate content that is upsetting and leads to emotional distress and/or trauma. Content can influence all spheres of life including family, current and future employment and social life.
- *Contact*: Cyber-harassment can lead to offline actions involving contact, including physical, psychological and verbal violence.
- *Conduct*: People change their behaviour as a consequence of cyber-hate content, for example, being afraid to go out, sometimes leading to self-harming behaviours when they are vulnerable, such as visiting self-harm and suicide websites.

Awan and Zempi (2016) found that women were disproportionately targeted in Muslim hate crime online (see also Tell MAMA, 2014; Citron, 2014). Impacts on these women were profound, including being afraid to go out of their own homes, being fearful in public places such as supermarkets and ceasing to go online for fear of experiencing hate content. This mirrors offline Muslim hate crimes, while other hate crimes tend to have more male victims, underlining the importance of developing gender-sensitive responses. The threat of suicide is particularly relevant to transgender and disability hate crime (see Box 2.3) and is a further example of the way in which on/offline hate crimes can connect to extend the reach and severity of impacts given the easy access to suicide websites.

Box 2.3: Suicidal ideation as a hate crime impact

"I know from experience what a risk of serious harm is to a trans person, because I know the impact that minor, accumulative offences have. The impact increases the risk of serious harm to a trans person because it reduces confidence and increases risk of suicide. One hundred incidents can have more impact than one physical assault. I would prefer someone to beat seven bells out of me and I can spend a couple of days in hospital than actually go through the daily rubbish which I've been through." (Victim of transgender hate crime, South Wales, quoted in Williams and Tregidga, 2014: 959)

"I've been in work sometimes and been really upset and you feel like jumping off a cliff or hanging yourself or something because no one is helping you." (Victim of disability hate crime, Gwent, quoted in Williams and Tregidga, 2014: 959)

How can practitioners help?

True Vision is an online site owned by the Association of Chief Police Officers (ACPO) and provides helpful information on how to respond to cyber-hate. It advises victims to report the abuse or offensive content to the website administrator (use a 'report this' button on the website if there is one) and/or report it to the hosting company. Content should be reported to the police if it matches the definition of illegal content (see Box 2.4).

Box 2.4: Illegal hate content

Inciting hatred

In England and Wales, it can be an offence to stir up hatred on the grounds of:

- race;
- religion; and
- sexual orientation.

(There is no similar offence relating to disability or transgender.)

Other offences

The content of a website can also be illegal when it threatens or harasses a person or a group of people. If this is posted because of hostility based on race, religion, sexual orientation, disability or transgender, then we consider it to be a hate crime.

Illegal material could be in words, pictures, videos and even music and could include:

- messages calling for racial or religious violence;
- web pages with pictures, videos or descriptions that glorify violence against anyone due to their race, religion, disability, sexual orientation or because they are transgender; and
- chat forums where people ask other people to commit hate crimes.

Source: True Vision, see: http://www.report-it.org.uk/reporting_internet_hate_crime

---

However, there cannot be an assumption that the client can immediately go online to make a complaint. When a client tells a practitioner about online abuse and harassment, they may feel completely disempowered and afraid to do anything online. The casework relationship is crucial to gradually empower victims to begin to feel safe again on- and offline. Help is needed to build confidence and support the client to work together to make a complaint to the information technology (IT) company or to report it to the police.

Online abuse can be as damaging as offline hate crime and can be extremely difficult to avoid as the internet infiltrates many areas of a person's life through a multitude of devices. It will be important to listen to how the client feels and to explore how the impacts have affected them at home, school, work and in their social (media) life.

Promoting digital citizenship

Internet intermediaries, such as Internet Service Providers (ISPs), website hosts and IT companies, have a key role in countering cyberhate (Citron and Norton, 2011). Facebook, Twitter, Google, YouTube and Microsoft have supported the development of a European code of conduct with the European Commission (2016). This requires:

* IT companies to review the majority of valid notifications for the removal of illegal hate speech in less than 24 hours and, if necessary, to remove or disable access to such content;
* IT companies to intensify their work with civil society organisations (CSOs) to deliver best practice training on countering hateful rhetoric and prejudice, and to increase the scale of their proactive outreach to CSOs to help them deliver effective counter-speech campaigns; and
* IT companies to make information about 'trusted reporters' available on their websites.

On the basis of this code of conduct, practitioners can:

* ensure that cyber-hate is reported to IT companies, wherever it occurs;
* check that the hate speech has been removed within 24 hours;
* look out for and request training from IT companies for their agency and others in their community;
* get involved in counter-speech campaigns (see Box 2.5); and
* become a 'trusted reporter' of cyber-hate.

Practitioners do not need to be experts, but in responding to online abuse and harassment, it will be helpful to upskill in digital literacy to empower victims to regain security and safety, or have access to technical support when needed. The South West Grid for Learning has some excellent, freely available digital literacy resources, including developing skills for managing digital privacy and security, self-image and identity, digital footprint and reputation, and cyber-bullying (see: http://www.digital-literacy.org.uk/Curriculum-Overview.aspx).

Box 2.5: Creating counter-hate speech

In 2004, the number-one Google result for a search of 'jew' was the URL jewwatch. com, a site featuring anti-Semitic content. In response, a Jewish activist asked people around the Web to link the word 'Jew' to a Wikipedia article so that search engine users would more likely see that article at the top of search results rather than the Jew Watch site, a practice known as a 'Googlebomb'. Neo-Nazi sites, in turn, launched a counter-Googlebomb, leading the results back to Jew Watch. Individuals asked Google to remove Jew Watch entirely from its search results. Google announced that it would not change its software ... [but] inserted its own advertisement entitled 'Offensive Search Results' on top of its page where the link to Jew Watch appeared. (Citron and Norton, 2011: 1471-2)

Summary

The internet can be a force for good as well as harm. The digital world has extended the reach of hate crime and the capacity for perpetrators to expand their activities both on- and offline, and impacts can be severe. While addressing the problem of cyber-hate is complex, the basic principles of victim support cut across both on- and offline worlds. Chapter Three focuses on the minimum service standards that hate crime victims have a right to request and receive when reporting and being supported.

RIGHTS-BASED SUPPORT FRAMEWORKS

Recognising and responding to the specific needs of hate crime victims has, in recent years, entered the policy domain across the European Union (EU) and within the UK, particularly in relation to providing minimum service standards of victim support. This has been the result of long-term grass-roots campaigning for hate crime victims to be appropriately recognised and responded to by service providers, including the police and victim support services.

Victim support services have existed in Europe for over 30 years, and the first service was set up in the UK in 1974. In the year 2014/15, Victim Support offered help to 1.2 million people affected by crime in England and Wales (see: www.victimsupport.org.uk). The EU Agency for Fundamental Rights (FRA, 2014) defines a victim support service as one that provides assistance available to victims before, during and after criminal proceedings, including emotional and psychological support, as well as advice relating to legal, financial and practical matters. This is potentially a wide range of services that a victim may access and that a caseworker may need to navigate.

EU member states are less advanced in the field of support for hate crime victims in comparison to other categories of crimes (FRA, 2014). Indeed, EU-wide research of member states (FRA, 2016), with 263 professionals from the criminal justice system and non-government organisations (NGOs) supporting hate crime victims, found that:

- almost nine out of 10 interviewed professionals believe that measures are needed to improve hate crime victims' awareness of their rights and of the victim support services available to them as victims of hate crime;
- six out of 10 interviewees view the actual lack of support services as a factor that impedes victims' access to justice;
- hate crime services are patchy and fragmented;
- trust in the police is low;
- there is a lack of commitment to identify, prosecute and impose sentences for hate crime; and
- hate crime needs to be taken more seriously by the police and judiciary.

Given that the under-reporting of hate crime is a recognised concern, when a victim does report, they should, at a minimum, be told their rights and what they can expect from the police and other agencies during the course of the complaint. This is not always happening and can further disempower and disenchant victims from coming forward and reporting. Recent developments in the EU and UK in recognising the minimum needs of and service standards for victims is a positive contribution to the casework practice of hate crime advocates working with the criminal justice system. These standards provide a framework and transparency that begin to make criminal justice accountable to victims.

The European Union Victims' Directive

Prior to 2012, the rights of victims of crime varied from one member state to another without any agreed minimum standards for victims across the EU (McDonald, 2012). Directive 2012/29/EU of the European Parliament and of the Council establishing minimum standards for the rights, support and protection of victims of crime was introduced to provide consistency (European Commission, 2012). Each EU member state was required to implement the provisions of the Directive into their national laws by 16 November 2015.

The Directive, also known as the Victims' Directive, is an EU law that brings significant added value compared to the previous legal framework since it contains more concrete and comprehensive rights for victims and clearer obligations for member states. The Directive recognises that victims of crime have a range of needs, varying from victim to victim. To meet these different needs, it is necessary that all victims are treated individually. The Directive identifies that the needs of victims can be grouped in five broad categories:

- *respectful treatment* and *recognition* as victims, both within the justice system and more widely by society;
- *protection* both from intimidation, retaliation and further harm by the accused or suspected, and from harm during criminal investigations and court proceedings, such as by avoiding the repeated interviewing of the victim;
- *support*, including immediate assistance following a crime, longer-term physical and psychological assistance, and practical assistance during proceedings to help victims understand and participate, as well as to reduce their distress;
- *access to justice* to ensure that victims are aware of their rights and understand them both linguistically and legally, are able to provide additional information, and are able to participate in proceedings; and
- *compensation* and *restoration*, whether through financial damages paid by the state or by the offender, or through mediation or other forms of restorative justice that allow victims to face the accused with a view to reaching a voluntary agreement between them on how to repair the harm to the victim.

New rights and obligations

New rights and obligations established by the EU Victims' Directive include the following:

- *Family members* of deceased victims are defined as victims and benefit from all rights in the Directive; family members of surviving victims have the right to support and protection. Family members are widely defined and also include non-married intimate partners.
- *Accessible and understandable information* – all communication with victims must be made in a way that victims understand (linguistically or otherwise); an emphasis is made on child-sensitive communication.
- *Access to victim support* – member states must ensure access for victims and their family members to general victim support and specialist support, in accordance with their needs. The Directive specifies the basic level of services that need to be provided. Support is not dependent on the victim having reported the crime. Member states must facilitate referrals from police to victim support organisations.
- *Specialist support services* must, as a minimum, provide shelters and targeted and integrated support for victims with specific needs, such as victims of sexual violence, victims of gender-based violence and victims of violence in close relationships, including trauma support and counselling.
- *Review decisions not to prosecute* – victims have the right to be informed about a decision not to proceed with prosecution of the offender and will also have the entirely new right to have such a decision reviewed.
- *Individual assessment to identify vulnerability and special protection measures* – all victims will be individually assessed to determine whether they are vulnerable to secondary or repeat victimisation or intimidation during criminal proceedings. If they have specific needs, a whole range of special measures will be put in place to protect them. Children are always presumed vulnerable and particular attention will be paid to some categories of victims, which include hate crime, disabled victims, gender-based violence and violence in close relationships, sexual violence or exploitation.

Strengthened rights and obligations

Rights and obligations strengthened by the EU Victims' Directive include the following:

- *Information rights* – victims will receive a range of information from first contact with authorities. Victims will also receive information about their case, including a decision to end the investigation, not to prosecute and the final judgement (including the reasons for such decisions), and information on the time and place of the trial and the nature of the criminal charges.
- *Interpretation and translation* – during criminal proceedings, victims with an active role have the right to interpretation and translation to enable their participation. Victims can challenge a decision not to receive interpretation and translation. All victims will receive a translation of the acknowledgement of their complaint.
- *Protection of all victims is reinforced* – the privacy of victims and their family members must be respected and contact with the offender avoided (all new court buildings must have separate waiting areas).
- *Restorative justice safeguards* – victims who choose to participate in restorative justice processes (referred to as mediation in the Framework Decision) must have access to safe and competent restorative justice services, subject to some minimum conditions set out in the Directive.
- *Training of practitioners* has become an obligation and emphasis is also put on cooperation between member states and at the national level, as well as awareness raising about victims' rights.

Significance of Articles 22 and 23 to hate crimes

Schweppe (2013) highlights that Articles 22 and 23 of the Directive are of particular significance to hate crimes. Article 22(1) states that, in assessing the needs of victims, an assessment must be carried out to determine if the victim has any particular 'protection needs' and the extent to which they would benefit from 'special measures' in the course of criminal proceedings 'due to their particular vulnerability to secondary and repeat victimisation, to intimidation and to retaliation'. In this context, Article 22(2) states that the assessment should take the personal characteristics of the victim, the nature of the crime and the circumstances of the crime into account.

Article 22(3) states that *particular attention* should be paid to victims who 'have suffered a crime committed with a bias or discriminatory motive, which could notably be related to their personal characteristics'. Hate crime victims 'shall be *duly considered*'. The Directive states in Article 23(2) that the 'particular attention' to be paid to victims in criminal investigations includes the following:

- interviews with the victim should be carried out in premises designed or adapted for that purpose;
- interviews with the victim should be carried out by or through professionals trained for that purpose;
- all interviews with the victim should be conducted by the same persons unless this is contrary to the good administration of justice; and
- all interviews with victims of sexual violence, gender-based violence or violence in close relationships, unless conducted by a prosecutor or a judge, should be conducted by a person of the same sex as the victim, if the victim so wishes, provided that the course of the criminal proceedings will not be prejudiced.

Definition of hate crime

The Directive adopts a broad and inclusive definition of hate crimes. Once a crime is committed with a bias or discriminatory motive *related to their personal characteristics*, the question of specific protection arises. The Directive does not require all hate crime legislation to adopt this definition, but offers a two-tiered approach to victims of hate crimes:

- The Directive will apply to those victims already covered by domestic legislation (if it exists).

- The Directive's broadness may mean that it is also applicable to victims of a hate crime who are targeted based on a bias that is not included under existing hate crime laws (eg in England and Wales, age, appearance or gender). For this latter category of victim, the base crime will be prosecuted normally, though the victim may be entitled to the 'particular attention' that the Directive requires (Schweppe, 2013).

Code of Practice for Victims of Crime (England and Wales)

The Code of Practice for Victims of Crime forms a key part of the wider UK government strategy to transform the criminal justice system by putting victims first and making the system more responsive and easier to navigate (Ministry of Justice, 2015: 1). The Code requires a range of organisations to provide services to victims that hate crime caseworkers will work with. These include the Crown Prosecution Service, police and crime commissioners, all police forces in England and Wales (including British Transport Police) and witness care units (Ministry of Justice, 2015: 2). Victim support services are not covered by this Code.

The Code states that victims of crime:

- should be treated in a respectful, sensitive, tailored and professional manner without discrimination of any kind;
- should receive appropriate support to help them, as far as possible, to cope and recover;
- should be protected from re-victimisation;
- should know what information and support is available to them from reporting a crime onwards; and
- should know who to request help from if they are not getting it (Ministry of Justice, 2015: 1).

Hate crime victims and enhanced entitlements

As they are more likely to require enhanced support and services through the criminal justice process, the Code sets out enhanced entitlements for victims in the following categories:

- victims of the most serious crime;
- persistently targeted victims; and
- vulnerable or intimidated victims.

The Code states that victims of the most serious crime, including hate crime victims, are eligible for enhanced entitlements. Although not explicitly stated, hate crime victims are also likely to feature in the other two categories. Hate crime victims have often been persistently targeted. The Code defines 'persistently targeted victims' as:

If you have been targeted repeatedly as a direct victim of crime over a period of time, particularly if you have been deliberately targeted or you are a victim of a sustained campaign of harassment or stalking. (Ministry of Justice, 2015: 14)

The Code defines 'vulnerable or intimidated victims' through a range of criteria, including being under 18 at the time of the offence, having a physical disability and having an impairment of intelligence and social functioning.

The Code further states that an intimidated victim is eligible for enhanced entitlements if the service provider considers that the quality of the evidence will be affected because of fear or distress about testifying in court. In making this assessment, the service provider has to take into account a number of factors, including the victim's age and, if relevant, the victim's social and cultural background, religious beliefs or political opinions, ethnic origin, and domestic and employment circumstance (Ministry of Justice, 2015: 14). Hate crime victims will be included in this assessment.

Box 3.1: Minimum expectations from the police

The Code of Practice for Victims of Crime states that the police must provide all victims with at least the following responses:

- A written acknowledgement that a crime has been reported, including the basic details of the offence.
- Where the police consider that there may be a risk of harm to the victim, they may agree with the victim not to send a written acknowledgement.
- A clear explanation of what to expect from the criminal justice system when a crime has been reported or the victim is contacted during the investigations.
- An assessment of whether the victim wants support, as well as what type of support and help. This will help to assess whether the victim is in one of the three identified categories of victim who may need enhanced support.
- To be informed as to how often updates on the status of the case will be received.
- An explanation within five working days of a decision not to investigate a crime.
- To explain that the victim's details will be automatically passed to victim support services within two working days of reporting the crime. The victim can ask for their details not to be passed on.
- The victim is entitled to receive information about victim support services, including contact details from the police so that they can access their support at any time.
- To be advised when an investigation into the case has been concluded with no person being charged and to have the reasons explained to the victim.

Source: Ministry of Justice (2015: 20).

The Code of Practice for Victims of Crime provides a transparent approach to the responses of the police (see Box 3.1) after a crime has been reported and enables a caseworker to work with and make accountable agencies within the criminal justice system to ensure that the needs and rights of a hate crime victim are met and responded to. Victim Support Europe advocates that a hate crime victim (see also Box 3.2):

- has access to the rights given by the EU Directive;
- is efficiently referred to victim support services;
- has their individual needs assessed and met throughout the criminal justice process by trained professionals;
- can count on the delivery of victim support services;
- is granted minimum standards of procedural rights; and
- may benefit from good cooperation between criminal justice agencies and victim support organisations.

Box 3.2: Minimum standards for hate crime support

Behaviour towards the client	Service-based responses
Believe the client, do not question the validity of the client's account and do not blame the client for what they have experienced.	There should be no hierarchy of victims; instead, the services are provided regardless of the personal characteristics and nature of the crime.
Communicate through a framework of respect and dignity, for example, give clients enough time to talk and to articulate their experiences and needs, and demonstrate that they are being listened to.	Keep clients involved and informed in the case as it progresses through the criminal justice system. The victim should not be forgotten through the criminal justice system or complaint process.
Respond to the client as an individual and not with a preconceived set of assumptions. Crime impacts differently on every victim and the client will need someone who can understand their particular needs, which are acknowledged and addressed.	Set clear expectations of what can be achieved and what a caseworker can and cannot do for them.

3. RIGHTS-BASED SUPPORT FRAMEWORKS

It is the right of the victim to receive information and not to be made responsible for the practicalities surrounding its delivery. As a minimum, service providers should tell the victim what information is available and ask whether they want access to it.	Service providers should have up-to-date information available about relevant services for clients and the rights that they have access to.
Victims have the right to be understood and communicate their needs. Information should be delivered in a language and manner that the victim can understand.	Consideration should be given to the victim's communication skills and any language requirements. Vital documents should be translated into a language spoken by the client. If required, the victim should be able to access interpreters, free of charge, when receiving support services and during police interviews or questioning in court.
The victim has a right to know who to contact to receive more information or ask any further questions regarding the case or the process.	Provide the client with relevant contact details of all the agencies involved in the case.
Clients can expect to be recognised and treated in a respectful, sensitive and professional manner, without discrimination of any kind.	Crime is a violation of a victim's fundamental rights and service providers have to limit additional harm or victimisation due to unsuitable questions and behaviours. Appropriate training should be provided to all who have contact with a victim. Training should include the impact of crime, coping strategies, avoiding intimidation, repeat and secondary victimisation, and the availability and relevance of victim support services.

Source: Adapted from Victim Support Europe (2013).

Victim Personal Statements

The UK government action plan on hate crime (Home Office, 2016) wants to encourage and improve the use of the Victim Personal Statement (VPS) to ensure that hate crime victims have their voices and experiences heard. The Crown Prosecution Service will produce new guidance on community impact statements that recognise and reflect how hate crime can have an impact beyond individual victims.

The Victim Personal Statement gives victims an opportunity to describe the wider effects of the crime upon them, express their concerns and highlight whether or not they require support (see Crown Prosecution Service, no date). A VPS can only be used when a case goes to court and a person either pleads guilty or is found guilty.

Summary

The EU Directive is an opportunity for all EU member states to fulfil their obligations to meeting the identified rights of victims. However, challenges that crime victims face include the following:

- the position of victims still needs to be improved;
- victims of crime continue to be met with societal prejudice and stereotypes;
- victims' behaviour is often scrutinised to see if they are (at least in part) to blame for their victimisation; and
- these attitudes and behaviours are likely to be even worse in crimes that are primarily under-reported, like hate crime (Victim Support Europe, no date).

The rights-based support framework informs a caseworker of the minimum level of service that a hate crime victim has the right to receive from different service providers. Chapter Four focuses on the needs of hate crime victims and how service providers can meet these needs.

THE VICTIM'S PERSPECTIVE

Hate crime is an attack on an individual's actual or perceived identity or identities. As such, it is recognised that the consequences of hate crime can have longer-lasting impacts than non-hate crime (Iganski, 2008; Kees et al, 2016). There is a range of groups that are potential victims of hate crime, for example, migrants or refugees, Muslim women, disabled people, and gypsies, Travellers and Roma. Their relative stigmatised position in society means that their knowledge of, experience of and access to services will range from familiarity to fear. For example, in some circumstances, the police may be seen as enforcers of a political regime by those who have or are escaping persecution as opposed to an agency mandated to investigate a complaint and uphold due process. Similarly, negative experiences of service providers, more generally, but particularly the police, may result in victims of hate crime feeling less confident that they will be believed and taken seriously or that there will be action (ODIHR, 2009).

Recognising needs and acknowledging the rights of hate crime victims requires practitioners to work from a perspective that makes the client a visible and active participant in their complaint. Following the victim's perspective is a set of principles, skills and behaviours that are learnt through active casework practice and can have tangible positive outcomes in the lives of marginalised groups and individuals.

Working with and supporting hate crime victims is something that requires more than a common-sense approach, knowledge of the law and partnerships with relevant agencies. Although these are important, casework practice requires: recognition of the experiences of hate crime victims; transparent values that influence the behaviours of the practitioner; interpersonal skills and knowledge that are learned and practised; and an ability to respond to the particular circumstances and demands that a client may make on caseworkers. Understanding and responding from the victim's perspective is a critical aspect of hate crime casework practice.

Moving away from 'the ideal victim'

Victims and victim movements, including hate crime victims, have a much higher public profile within policy, legal and academic discourse than ever before. The increasing visibility of the rights and needs of victims of crime has been a 'lengthy process' and is the result of various factors (Dignan, 2005), including: the role of the media; a growing sensitisation through the 1960s and 1970s to the needs of particular vulnerable groups, particularly domestic violence and sexual abuse; use of victim surveys to measure the extent and impact of crime; and the higher public profile given to well-publicised incidents. All of these have also been important to hate crime being firmly placed in the public and policy arena.

The political and community struggles to recognise hate crime victims as deserving of recognition as legitimate complainants has evolved over a long period of community-based struggles (Newham Monitoring project, 2000). For many years, hate crime victims did not fit Christie's (1986) stereotyped construct of what '*the ideal victim*' is. The ideal victim is 'a person or category of individuals who – when hit by crime – most readily are given the complete and legitimate status of being a victim' (Christie, 1986: 18). To achieve this ideal status, Christie identified a number of attributes including: the victim is weak in relation to the offender; the victim is blameless; the victim does not know the stranger; and, crucially, 'the victim has the right combination of power, influence or sympathy to successfully elicit victim status without threatening (and thus risking opposition from) strong countervailing vested interests' (Dignan, 2005: 17).

It took the murder of a defenceless young black man in South East London in 1993 to change public perceptions of the long history of race hate-motivated violence and murders and for it to be seen in its proper context of being fuelled by bias, prejudice and racism. The racist murder of Stephen Lawrence, the resulting campaign by the Lawrence family for justice and the public inquiry (the Stephen Lawrence Inquiry) into the police mismanagement of the murder investigation (Macpherson, 1999) sadly illustrates what can occur in practice when crime victims are categorised as ideal or having un/deserving status. The Inquiry highlighted the neglect and prejudicial suspicion that the Metropolitan Police officers operated from at the scene of the racist attack where Stephen Lawrence and his friend Dwayne Brooks were assaulted and attacked. Rather than showing a duty of care towards the victims, the police officers treated both the victims with suspicion and as potential offenders. The Metropolitan Police were accused of institutional racism and the Macpherson Report offered a range of recommendations to change policy, practice and the law.

Prior to the Macpherson Report, all UK police forces recorded racist incidents using an asymmetrical definition adopted in 1985 by the Association of Chief Police Officers (ACPO), which read:

> *any incident in which it appears to the reporting or investigating officer that the complaint involves an element of racial motivation; or any incident which includes an allegation of racial motivation made by any person.* (Chahal, 1992)

The Macpherson Inquiry offered a new working definition of a 'racist incident':

> *any incident which is perceived to be racist by the victim or any other person.* (Macpherson, 1999: 328)

This definition was a shift away from a criminal justice-centred definition of a racist incident, where the primary decision-maker was a police officer, and towards a victim-centred definition (Goodey, 2011:

427). The new definition shifted the balance of power so that when a complaint is made to, for example, the police, a housing officer or a teacher, the experiences and perception of the victim are central at the outset. This aimed to challenge the long-standing experiences of hate crime victims, for example, of not feeling that they will be believed or taken seriously when reporting to an official authority, fear and mistrust of the police, and fear of disclosure of sexual orientation or immigration status (Chahal and Julienne, 1999; Chahal, 2003; ODIHR, 2009; Kees et al, 2016).

What is the victim's perspective?

A definition of the victim's perspective developed by European-wide hate crime service providers is:

> The victim's perspective means we will believe, listen, make visible and give a voice to the client's experience. We will behave professionally, be open and honest about what we can realistically achieve together with our clients. We will work with the client to provide practical, emotional and legal support and options, signposting to other services and developing strategies that aim to ensure their safety. Support and advocacy services will recognise and understand the impact of discrimination and disadvantage at local community, institutional and society level and contribute to preventing hate crime through awareness raising and campaigning. (Kees et al, 2016: 27)

The casework approach that stems from this definition asks practitioners to recognise that:

- being a victim of hate crime is part of being a discriminated group;
- the victim's experience and perspective is lost or neglected because of being made invisible through discrimination;
- the victim themselves may not know they are a victim of hate crime;
- the victim may be worried/fear reactions/reprisal if they report to an official agency;

- the victim may feel ashamed about what is happening to them;
- they may want to move/not go back to where they live because of the victimisation; and
- working from a victim's perspective has wider implications for challenging discrimination, harassment and violence through training, campaigning and lobbying in the wider community and society (Kees et al, 2016).

Working from the victim's perspective recognises the unequal power balance between the victim and the perpetrator, as well as the victim and the reporting agency. It foregrounds a person-centred or person-oriented approach that aims to challenge the marginalisation of victims more generally, and hate crime victims in particular. Further, it recognises the interests of the victim as a primary responsibility.

The caseworker who has first contact with a hate crime victim or witness has a responsibility and duty of care towards that person. At the initial point of contact, little, if anything, is known about the circumstances and experiences of the victim. It is well documented that hate crime is under-reported and that victims are likely to be particularly vulnerable to secondary and repeat victimisation, intimidation and retaliation (FRA, 2014: 77). Working from a perspective that recognises the status of the victim as in need includes: 'recognising and acknowledging the validity of the account of the person who has suffered hate violence' (Kees et al, 2016: 27); recognising that they are in need of support and assistance that is appropriate; and moving towards establishing 'victim-related normative prescriptions' (Van Boven, 2013) of working with and recognising hate crime victims.

Victim's perspective as a protective factor

The current UK government's action plan against hate crime recognises that the available evidence suggests that hate crime victims are more likely to suffer repeat victimisation, more likely to suffer serious psychological impacts as a result and less likely than the victims of other crime to be satisfied with the police response (Home Office, 2016). A focused victim–oriented service must be able to offset these aggravating factors by being aware of protective factors.

Protective factors can be best demonstrated when positioning the recognised needs of the victim against the process of legal systems. Herman (2005: 574) argues that the wishes and needs of victims are often diametrically opposed to the requirements of legal proceedings. Box 4.1 highlights the needs of victims of crime and the requirements of legal systems from victims as witnesses.

Box 4.1: The needs of victims and legal systems

The needs of victims	The requirements of legal systems
Victims need social acknowledgement and support.	The court requires victims to endure a public challenge to their credibility.
Victims need to establish a sense of power and control over their lives.	The court requires victims to submit to a complex set of rules and bureaucratic procedures that they may not understand and over which they have no control.
Victims need an opportunity to tell their stories in their own way, and in a setting of their own choice.	The court requires them to respond to a set of yes-or-no questions that break down any personal attempt to construct a coherent and meaningful narrative.
Victims often need to control or limit their exposure to specific reminders of the trauma.	The court requires them to relive the experience.
Victims often fear direct confrontation with their perpetrators.	The court requires a face-to-face confrontation between a complaining witness and the accused.

Source: Adapted from Herman (2005: 574).

Repeat and secondary victimisation

Repeat victimisation refers to the repeated victimisation of a person, household, place or property of the same type of any hate crime more than once during a year. The Crime Survey for England and Wales (CSEW) has found that there are higher rates of repeat victimisation for hate crime victims compared with crime overall, as well as for both personal and household crime (Corcoran et al, 2015: 17). If victims are choosing not to report to the police, then it is likely that the impacts will be greater on them, and when a report is made, it is often because they have reached a crisis point (see Chapter Six). Chahal and Julienne (1999) found that reporting is a strategy when the hate victimisation has become intolerable and life-threatening, or where there has been serious property damage or assault. A victim who does report or approach a service may have experienced multiple incidents and will want an appropriate and professional service that prioritises support to deal with the immediate consequences of the hate violence, as well as to be believed and treated with dignity (Chahal, 2003; Chakraborti and Hardy, 2016; Kees et al, 2016).

Service providers should be aware of how organisational and professional practices and responses can impact negatively on the victim and should aim to avoid the secondary victimisation of victims, defined as follows:

> *Secondary victimisation involves a lack of understanding of the suffering of victims which can leave them feeling both isolated and insecure. The experience of secondary victimisation intensifies the immediate consequences of crime by prolonging or aggravating the victim's trauma … can leave victims feeling alienated from society as a whole.* (European Forum for Victim Services, no date)

Working from a victim's perspective

A hate crime caseworker's role is to provide assistance, advice and support that contribute to the client's problem being resolved. A victim-centred approach involves at least the attributes identified in the following (Chahal, 2003, 2008; Chakraborti and Hardy, 2016; Kees et al, 2016).

Validation

The expectation from a client is that he or she is believed and that their experiences are validated through being listened to, being heard, being treated with kindness and respect, immediate action being taken to support the victim, and responding to the complaint. Validation includes an acknowledgement of the basic facts of the crime from formal authorities and an acknowledgement of harm (Herman, 2005). Caseworkers are not always able to end the hate violence, but their professional approach towards the client, the complaint and working with other agencies contributes towards a client knowing that they have received an appropriate and professional service. Crucially, validation also includes vindication from the community, which includes the victim wanting the offense to be condemned by society and for the perpetrators to be accountable for their actions (Herman, 2005: 597).

Non-judgemental approach

Clients entering a casework service want to be assured of an empathic and non-judgemental hearing of their experiences. Where appropriate, this may include partiality, which is characterised by solidarity towards and acceptance of the client's experiences without compromising the integrity of the investigative process (Kees et al, 2016).

Partiality and neutral approaches

Independent hate crime advocacy and support services will take a position of partiality towards the client and advocate fully on their behalf. However, some practitioners who work with hate crime victims will take a position that is influenced or dependent by their own organisational position in relation to the client and the alleged perpetrator. For example, a social housing provider, the police and an educational institution will be organisationally positioned to listen, collect information and respond to both the victim and the alleged perpetrator and to take action based on the evidence gathered. They are not 'partial' actors, but will be required to take a position of being neutral and free from bias. The limits of support and partiality should be communicated to victims.

Emotional support

Offering immediate and ongoing support helps clients feel comfortable, listened to and responded to. Caseworkers will have to both manage and respond to the emotional fallout of hate crime and be able to offer support which indicates that they understand, are willing to listen and engage with the issues that the client is presenting, or be able to signpost to a service who can respond to the effects of post-victimisation symptoms.

Advocacy

Advocating on behalf of a client means that the caseworker begins to share the burden of their client's experience and can begin to represent them and co-produce strategies that problem-solve and contribute to empowerment. This has to be clearly communicated and agreed with the client as the relationship develops. Being an advocate on behalf of a client may occur in the early stages of a complaint or on an ongoing basis for more vulnerable victims.

Problem solving

The process of casework will problem-solve with the client to produce realistic actions and timescales, and to make agreements of what will happen next and by whom. Problem solving will include considering the financial costs, for example, of additional security, damage to property, medical documentation and accessing other relevant services for welfare benefits or the complexities of immigration status.

Accessible service

An accessible service is crucial to responding from a person-centred approach. This can mean, for example, having regular updates about the progress of a case, having access to a caseworker via a direct telephone line or simply being listened to when emotionally distressed. However, it also means that buildings and places where a caseworker will meet a client are appropriate for the needs of a client. Accessibility offers a level of reassurance that the client's case is being progressed, that support is on hand if needed and that considerations have been made for the range of needs that a client may have.

Focus of a dedicated agency

Clients want a single agency or an individual to support them and be a point of contact. This enables continuity of contact with a dedicated and named person and builds a relationship of trust with the caseworker and the service.

Promoting rights

Offering information about the rights that clients have, the minimum service standards that they can expect, who to approach and what questions to ask can help them when dealing with other agencies.

Signposting

Providing appropriate information and referring to other relevant agencies, including specialist services, for example, psychological support or a friendly lawyer, empowers clients to make informed decisions about where and to whom they want to take their complaint and who can and should be involved in the process.

Aftercare

Closing a case with the client's permission and making contact with them after an agreed time lag provides reassurance that there is still support available, if needed.

Limits of casework and client satisfaction

All of the aforementioned are valued attributes for a casework support service, and highlight that a values-based service that puts the client at the centre of their service provision can be transformative. There are acknowledged limitations to casework practice that may have an impact on how a client views the services that they have received to help resolve their complaint.

Caseworkers and practitioners cannot end hate crime or everyday and systemic discrimination. Clients may also suffer both repeat and secondary victimisation and a complaint may not be recognised as a hate crime. Even if it is classified as a hate crime, the client may not receive justice from the criminal justice system and the problem may be ongoing after a range of interventions.

There may be a limitation on how many times and for how long a caseworker can work directly with a client. The client may not receive a good service from third-party providers or even key providers, like the police or the courts. Limited resources may mean that a client does not get information or an interpreter that meets their needs. A caseworker may leave their job and thus disrupt the continuity of service. The service may be closed down due to a lack of funding.

There may be trigger events (eg a terrorist attack) that increase spikes in the incidences and reporting of hate crime and stretch the resources of the service. The client may not follow through on agreed actions or may move away during the complaint. All these factors suggest that hate crime casework is complex and precarious.

However, practice-based research suggests that following a victim-oriented approach may result in hate crime clients both feeling and voicing a high level of satisfaction arising from the help and support that they have been given, even if the actual problem has not been resolved (Chahal, 2003). Box 4.2 summarises identified reasons for satisfaction and dissatisfaction (or areas for improvement) that clients with interpersonal problems have expressed.

Box 4.2: Reasons for client satisfaction and dissatisfaction with casework support

Client satisfaction	Client dissatisfaction
Had relief from unburdening (including experiencing the worker's approach as unhurried).	Clients and workers differed in perspective and attitude to problem solving and the understanding of the causes of problems.
Received emotional support (including listening and expending energy).	These differences were not recognised, acknowledged or explained.
Felt enlightenment (greater self-awareness, and improved understanding of their own situation).	The client felt that the worker doubted their story, was not interested in them or lacked authority to act.
Received guidance (suggestions, advice and recommendations).	Service providers were difficult to access or failed to communicate as agreed.
Access to support workers.	Lack of diversity in staff/volunteers.
Signposting to other services who may be able to help, including lawyers.	Problem not resolved and no other service has been offered.
The capacity to demonstrate empathy has been linked to positive outcomes for the client.	Lack of empathy has led to negative outcomes for the clients.

Source: Chahal (2003), Healy (2012), Mayer and Timms (1970) and Victim Support (2006).

Summary

A focus on a victim's perspective and the values that underpin it reminds a service provider to ensure that they have a set of standards and responses from which they can evidence their approach with clients. Following a victim's perspective recognises that what has been experienced is believed and the possible motivation for clients to report their experiences when they do is used in developing actions. This is important at an individual level because a victim coming forward and reporting hate crime must be taken seriously and believed. At a community level, service providers are able to provide evidence that authorities are accountable – that they recognise and will tackle hate crime. This may lead to an increase in the trust, confidence and satisfaction that is often lacking in clients when seeking help. Chapter Five builds on understanding the victim's perspective and identifies the role and principles that underpin hate crime casework and support.

ROLES AND PRINCIPLES OF CASEWORK SUPPORT

Having access to support services is fundamental to achieving justice for victims and ensuring that they know and can claim their rights. A hate crime support service provides a range of services, including advice, assistance and support, regardless of whether a crime has been committed or there are ongoing criminal proceedings (Chahal, 2003). A hate crime service will work with targeted groups, for example, a dedicated support service for lesbian, gay, bisexual and transgender (LGBT) victims of hate crime or potentially all groups of hate crime, while a generic victim support service is available to all victims of crime (eg Victim Support UK).

The role of hate crime casework

Hate crime casework is an interpersonal practice that involves understanding and responding to individuals to assist in resolving problems within their social environment. It is a purposeful and planned approach that achieves and creates change in how the individual engages with their social environment (Healy, 2012: 55–6).

Casework skills are different from counselling skills. Casework requires an interaction with and intervention in the wider social environment beyond listening and responding in private to the client, for example, working with the police or other third-party agencies to resolve a problem. There are three common approaches to casework practice that highlight the co-produced nature of this form of intervention:

- an emphasis on a staged approach to hate crime casework that begins with a comprehensive analysis of the problems or concerns to be addressed;
- collaboration with the client in establishing a clear shared understanding of the purpose of the relationship and the nature of the intervention; and
- recognition and enhancement of the client's capacities to address the challenges they face (see Healy, 2012: 55–7).

Hate crime casework is an interaction that makes clients aware of their rights, enabling them to take back control of their lives, and offers realistic expectations of the outcome of their complaint (Chahal, 2003).

The role of a hate crime practitioner is to develop a bounded working relationship over a period of time that reveals what the experiences and needs of the victim are, as well as to provide them with tools and resources to have the confidence and knowledge to respond to what they are experiencing. Box 5.1 identifies the key roles and responsibilities that are central to the function of hate crime casework support.

Box 5.1: Caseworker roles and responsibilities

- Advocacy that ensures a caseworker puts their skills, knowledge and experience at the disposal of, and will exercise them on behalf of, the client.
- Provide guidance but not influence; it is for the client to decide what their needs are.
- Empower clients to take decisions for themselves through providing advice and information, and offering choices.
- Fulfil a professional obligation to make sure that the client's complaints are resolved.
- Identify the individuals and agencies that can help and ensure that they fulfil their obligations.

- Have knowledge of the powers and responsibilities of individuals and agencies.
- Understand how a caseworker can ensure that other individuals and agencies use their powers swiftly and efficiently in the best interests of the client.
- Draw up a timetable for responding to the case in partnership with the client.
- Manage the case at all times in the client's best interests.
- Ensure that the client is satisfied that the case has been satisfactorily resolved.

Source: Adapted from Commission for Racial Equality (2000).

Multi-tasked and multi-skilled interventions

Hate crime caseworkers view their work as a multi-tasked and a multi-skilled intervention that involves working with victims and agencies, undertaking administrative duties (writing up notes, making telephone calls and sending emails, coordinating meetings with relevant professionals, and attending/leading hate crime case panels), and making representations.

Boundaries

Having professional boundaries is crucial to casework practice and the relationships that build with clients over time. These boundaries can be enhanced by caseworkers ensuring that they have:

- clarity of professional purpose;
- a primary focus on the needs and goals of the client; and
- clarity about the limits to the relationship, such as the fact that it is time-limited (Healy, 2012: 66).

Time

Time is an important factor in the casework relationship. People who have experienced trauma and who may not be familiar with recounting their experiences to strangers, whom they are meeting for the first time, may need time to talk and to articulate their needs (Kees et al, 2016: 24). This has to be balanced against the caseload of the practitioner, the complexity of the case and the actions that may be recommended.

Understanding the needs of the client

Hate crime caseworkers must ensure that the person being supported *feels* supported, has had time to consider all the available options and has decided what is in their own best interests. These basic requirements of the caseworker-client interaction will be achieved through listening to the complaint, gaining an understanding of the case and its effects from the perspective of the client. As a result of this interaction the caseworker will move forward with a co-produced plan of actions made with the client.

Principles-based casework

Hate crime casework support is a form of helping. Often, by the time many hate crime victims have officially reported what is happening to them, they have accessed a number of informal support mechanisms – family, friends, a doctor, a neighbour – and even attempted to solve the problem themselves. Reporting or seeking help from a hate crime practitioner often means that the victim has exhausted informal attempts at resolving their problem and needs immediate support, that there is an escalation of violence, or that the most recent attack is serious (Chahal and Julienne, 1999, Chahal 2003; Chakraborti et al, 2014). Key identified principles within the helping professions are helping, respect, empathy, diversity and intersectionality, and client empowerment (see Egan, 2014). To these, we can add anti-discriminatory practice and confidentiality.

Helping

Egan (2014) identifies the long history that 'helping' has had, primarily in a client–therapist relationship. However, helping outside of a therapeutic relationship is a cornerstone of the client–caseworker relationship. A client who has been a victim of hate crime is often seeking help, to be listened to and be believed within a supportive client-centred approach.

Carl Rogers introduced the client-centred approach to helping as a therapeutic model but it has wider applicability to hate crime casework. Rogers' approach highlighted an 'unconditional positive regard, accurate empathy and genuineness offered by the helper and perceived by the client' (Egan, 2014: 38). This client-centred approach generates 'a highly empathic relationship' that 'helped clients understand themselves, liberate their unused resources and manage their lives more effectively' (Egan, 2014: 38).

Helping is a practical relationship that enables the agency and resources of the client to be revealed and developed. Helping is an outcome-oriented process that relies on interaction, and on both the client and caseworker fulfilling agreed actions. Egan (2014) identifies four areas related to helping clients that can build a strong casework relationship:

- *Positive expectancies* – by providing a framework that helps clients understand the problems they are facing; by suggesting ways of dealing with the problems that the client is facing; and by building confidence in the client and the casework process.
- *Role* – by helping the client understand the details of the casework process. This may include expectations of each other, the frequency and length of meetings, and achieving agreed actions between meetings.
- *Goal formation* – helping as a goal is achieved by working towards life-enhancing outcomes chosen by the client.
- *Relationship flexibility* – different clients have different needs and there is no one-size-fits-all approach. The caseworker has to take their lead and direction from the client. The caseworker's approach will be governed by the client's response to the problem and how they present themselves and their needs in the meeting/interview.

Respect and acceptance

Egan (2014: 46) argues that respect is a foundation value 'on which all helping interventions are built'. Rogers (1957) defined respect as having 'positive regard', which includes a non-possessive warmth towards and affirmation of the client. This can include demonstrating kindness (Chakraborti and Hardy, 2016). Such behaviours demonstrated as normative practices are linked to successful client outcomes (Chahal, 2003; Egan, 2014). Normative behaviours that show respect to clients include the following:

- *Become competent and committed* – this refers to the caseworker being familiar with the values and skills required to be a successful practitioner. Building competency is as much learned from experience of casework practice as it is from shadowing others, becoming familiar with local service providers and their procedures for working with hate crime victims, and being a reflexive practitioner.
- *Be genuine and authentic* – to be genuine is to have a personal relationship with the client that is real and authentic. Authenticity is the capacity to relate to other people with personal integrity, to remain a 'real person' within the casework process and to maintain congruence between what we say, feel and do (Smale et al, 2000: 204). This means that hate crime caseworkers:
  - are honest about themselves, their organisational position, powers and responsibilities, resources, and limitations;
  - are self-aware of their values, behaviours and feelings; and
  - acknowledge any difficulties that they may have in working with difference, own their ignorance and confront their prejudices and biases (see Dhooper and Moore, 2000; Smale et al, 2000).
- *Be client-focused* – a caseworker's approach and actions will illustrate their attitude towards the client. The caseworker must enact the basic values of respect, acceptance and the victim's perspective in every aspect of the client–caseworker relationship. Being client-focused means taking a critical view. It does not mean always taking the

client's side, but means taking the points of view of clients seriously, challenging them where needed and keeping the client's agenda as the main focus (Egan, 2014: 47).

Empathy

Egan (2014: 48) highlights that respect is communicated through demonstrating empathy, which is 'the ability to understand the client from his or her point of view and, when appropriate, to communicate this understanding to the client'. Empathy is achieved when the client agrees with the practitioner's understanding of them. In other words, we begin to 'understand and feel the suffering of others even though we have never experienced that particular suffering ourselves' (Goodman, 2001). Empathy is crucial to effective hate crime casework and support, both to guide comprehension and for communicating compassion (Shebib, 2003).

Empathy is an important skill and strategy that humanises people and groups that have been dehumanised, depersonalised and denied due process. Hate crime is an exploitative relationship that justifies inferior treatment and the denial of empathetic opportunities, which 'erodes our capacity for empathy and thus the propensity for care and action' (Goodman, 2001: 127). Curry-Stevens (2011: 349) describes empathy-building as when 'people build a compassionate understanding of the distressing experiences of others. Empathy is typically evoked by telling stories of distress and making explicit links to the causes for distress'. In this respect, empathy is 'relationship-oriented' and co-produced through dialogue (Egan, 2014: 50). Key to responding to the needs of clients is to understand how the person's lived experience and context, as well as the cultural meaning of their dialogue, influence their thinking and feelings (Egan, 2014: 48–50).

Egan (2014) describes an empathic approach as a radical commitment that enables practitioners to understand clients from their point of view and through their lived experience. Empathy is also a reflexive practice in that the caseworker will need prior knowledge of the history and experience of the exclusion and discrimination of different groups but will also have to critically examine their approach to avoid stereotyping and ignoring an appreciation of diverse identities.

Acceptance of diversity and intersectionality

A caseworker is required to put to one side their own beliefs and views, and to work openly and genuinely with a client. Non-judgemental acceptance enables a caseworker to find a way to value and respect the client while not sharing all or any of their beliefs or values (Ellin, 2003). Hate crime caseworkers will need to be conscious of the range of groups that are recognised as potential victims of hate crime, the multiple identities that they may hold, and how these intersect with each other, with others and with wider cultural and societal norms: 'To provide professional hate crime victim support it is fundamental for caseworkers to constantly and critically reflect on their own social position in relation to the client and how this might impact upon their attitudes and actions' (Kees et al, 2016: 32).

Developing competencies that foreground the intersectionality of identities and interrelationship with diversity will enable caseworkers to communicate effectively and with empathy towards clients who are different from themselves. Diversity is the recognition and acceptance of both visible and hidden identities that a client holds, reveals and brings to the casework relationship. To effectively practice acceptance of diversity and intersectionality, caseworkers may consider:

- the power relationship within the casework relationship;
- their own values and biases towards others and difference;
- suppressing judgements and 'known' knowledge until the client reveals their identities;
- responding to each client as a new challenge and unique individual;
- recognising that there are no one-size-fits-all solutions ;
- being flexible to adapting communication style, building rapport and recognising gender-based issues;
- being accessible to clients in a variety of ways;

- reviewing whether your office space will meet the needs of the clients who may use it and what alternatives are available; and
- not being over-familiar with the client – the casework process is not about overly showing sympathy, but working towards empowerment.

The range of identities that people hold are not fixed entities, but multiple and fluid, which interact and shape how we are seen by others and how we experience the world around us. Hate crime victims may be targeted for victimisation not only because they are gay, for example, but also because they are black and/or disabled. Furthermore, groups identified as from the same protected characteristic may experience hate victimisation differently. For example, a Muslim woman's experience of hate crime might be different to that experienced by a Muslim man and, as such, the impact and effects may also be different.

Recent research has shown the interplay between religion, race and gender (Zempi and Awan, 2016), differences in experiences of hate crime based on sexual orientation and gender (Dick, 2008), and a perception and fear of the deliberate targeting of hate violence because of observable multiple identities and more than one protected characteristic (Chakraborti et al, 2014). Recognising the dynamics of intersectionality and multiple identities will enable a caseworker to provide an individual with an appropriate, empathic and empowering service.

Client empowerment

Empowerment is a complex, contested and multilayered concept (Thompson, 2011a). However, it is a process through which caseworkers 'can help clients discover, develop and use the untapped power within themselves' (Egan, 2014: 60), particularly given that hate crime has the ability to disempower, disrupt and impact adversely on the quality of life of its victims. Empowerment is a core value in hate crime casework practice and a caseworker can utilise elements of client empowerment, as identified in Box 5.2.

Box 5.2: Understanding client empowerment

- A process of helping people gain greater control over their lives and the socio-political and existential challenges they face (Thompson, 2011a).
- A process geared towards achieving authenticity that is about identifying the steps that need to be taken to remove obstacles to progress (Thompson, 2011a).
- Helping clients assess their resources realistically so that their aspirations do not outstrip their resources (Egan, 2014).
- Empowerment is not about seeing clients as victims or as fragile, but a two-way process that changes both the client and the caseworker (Egan, 2014).
- To achieve agency and self-responsibility in order to remove blocks and move forward.
- To contextualise how the client understands their problem and social situation, which is not based on assumptions or organisational policies and limitations.
- To identify all the possibilities that may meet the identified need, and to help the client come to decisions about their life (Payne, 1998).

Payne (1998: 276) highlights that implementing an empowerment strategy can be problematic for practitioners whose organisation is 'part of a social system which devalues certain minority groups'. Indeed, hate crime victims have themselves expressed a desire to be supported by independent, community-based hate crime services (Chahal, 2003). Further, Kees et al (2016) have suggested that a key aspect of the victim's perspective is 'partiality', namely, a caseworker offers support and help regardless of the client's legal, socio-economic and other social identities, and caseworkers do not work with the perpetrators of hate violence. Empowerment is about achieving social justice with the client, and certain agencies, for example, the police, are not mandated to empower or to be partial, but do have a duty to provide appropriate information, signpost and refer hate crime clients to available support services. Making clients aware of their rights is crucial to effective empowerment.

Anti-discriminatory practice

Each of us is unique, with individual rights, but we are also influenced and part of a wider social context. There is an increasing recognition of the need to take account of discrimination and how it impacts and affects life chances (Thompson, 2011a), and to understand and respond to the complexity of identity and diversity. In the UK, there are currently five legally recognised groups that are protected against forms of hate crime (disability, race, religion/faith, sexual orientation, transgender identity) and caseworkers are required to respond to each individual equally without prejudice.

Anti-discriminatory practice is practised within a set of values that promote equality and diversity, a belief in the dignity of the individual, and a wider recognition of how oppression and discrimination operate to exclude marginalised individuals and groups. The range of potential hate crime victims suggests that a caseworker has to embed anti-discriminatory practice in their reflective practice and recognise the level of vulnerability that a client has experienced and may feel, and the courage that it takes to make a complaint.

Confidentiality

The assurance of confidentiality is fundamental to casework and the ongoing relationship between the caseworker and client. The information is confidential between the client and the agency that the caseworker represents. Disclosing information and feelings about hate crime should be treated with respect; caseworkers should have due regard to any legal requirements for storing and sharing information and have informed consent from the client if referrals are being made and information is being shared with other relevant agencies.

Summary

As an interpersonal practice, hate crime casework has to deliver its services from a clear set of agreed principles and approaches that are communicated to the client and agencies. The role and principles attached to hate crime casework work towards empowering the client through a process that begins with an assessment and leads to creating a series of co-produced interventions. In Chapter Six, we will explore different but connected approaches to working with and supporting hate crime victims.

CASEWORK APPROACHES TO SUPPORTING CLIENTS

It is recognised in the research literature that reporting to an official agency, for example, the police, does happen but not necessarily immediately after the first hate incident. Hate crime is reported largely if there has been property damage or serious physical injury. By and large, verbal abuse, threats and harassment go unreported and the coping mechanism is often to ignore and avoid such experiences (Chahal and Julienne, 1999).

Some hate crime victims cope with little assistance after suffering victimisation (Craig-Henderson and Sloan, 2003), and some may not require any support, wanting to forget about it or seeing it as too trivial to report. Recent compelling research has identified that the hurts of hate crime are not uniformly experienced (Iganski and Lagou, 2015). People have different levels of resilience, coping mechanisms, support structures, familiarity with rights and reporting agencies, and, of course, identified needs. This chapter draws on three models of hate crime support that caseworkers are able to use with clients.

Crisis intervention

When an official complaint of hate crime is made it is often at the point of crisis:

> A crisis is a turning point, a situation which pushes our usual coping mechanisms beyond their limits of effectiveness and thus necessitates a different response, a different strategy for coping. (Thompson, 2011b: 1)

This turning point is the moment that a caseworker may first meet a client. The client may be in *crisis* and require an immediate response, for example, medical treatment or repairs to damaged property. The client's coping abilities may be lowered and they may be in emotional turmoil, fearful of further violence and concerned about their and their family's safety and security. These crisis points will generate reactions of immediacy in the client and a caseworker will have to untangle what can be achieved with the client. The client may have an expectation that the reporting agency or caseworker can respond to these *crises* straightaway. Crisis intervention in this context is to help the client in crisis to 'review or renegotiate certain aspects of their thoughts, feelings or intentions' (Thompson, 2011b: 18) because:

> what happens in a crisis is that our habitual strengths and ways of coping do not work; we fail to adjust either because the situation is new to us, or it has not been anticipated, or a series of events become too overwhelming. (Coulshed and Orme, 2006: 134, quoted in Trevithick, 2012: 320)

Crisis intervention recognises that a state of equilibrium has broken down and can be restored (Caplan, 1964). It emphasises the capacity of people to deal with problems and to be able to return to a steady state, which is dependent on three factors:

- people's internal psychological strengths and weaknesses;
- the nature of the problem faced; and
- the quality of the help provided (Trevithick, 2012: 320).

In applying crisis intervention to casework practice, first and foremost, clients have to be recognised as individuals and their experiences have to be listened to as unique. Second, it is a time-limited intervention (one to six weeks) and has a focused approach, which is particularly useful with hate crime victims who may report at a crisis point and require rights-based interventions that provide guidance, signposting, information and support over a limited period.

Crisis intervention aims to:

- mobilise appropriate support systems and resources, for example, through advocacy;
- offer the client in crisis a degree of calming reassurance and a temporary prop to their self-esteem and confidence through rapport and positive interest; and
- facilitate the learning of new and more effective coping mechanisms through other approaches to helping.

A caseworker cannot promise that their intervention will stop the hate violence (Chahal, 2003; Kees et al, 2016). However, they can offer and demonstrate that over a time-bounded period of crisis intervention casework, support and advocacy, they can help the client contribute to their own empowerment.

Crisis intervention model

There are different crisis intervention approaches available to help people cope positively with crises and feelings of disequilibrium. Crisis intervention models have a number of core features, which include an immediate assessment with the client using effective listening skills, building trust and rapport, identifying methods for coping such as resources they have that can be accessed or used, developing a plan, and follow-up contact with the client (Thompson, 2011b). Box 6.1 highlights one such model of crisis intervention called the SAFER-R Model, which aims to move the client from a state of crisis to achieving a baseline level of functionality.

Box 6.1: SAFER-R Model of crisis intervention

SAFER –R Model	Behaviours
Stabilise	• Explain your role and presence
	• Create a calm environment
	• Be professional
	• Assess impact of the immediate environment on the client
	• Build trust and rapport
	• Respond to immediate emergences
	• Establish immediacy – what do they need right now?
Acknowledge	• Offer words of support to help clients feel safe
	• Ask and listen to what has happened
	• Gather information
	• Be empathetic
	• Recognise silence
Facilitate understanding	• Focus on how the person feels
	• Validate their emotions
	• Paraphrase what they are saying
	• Normalise their symptoms
	• Attribute their reactions to the situation, not personal weakness
	• Establish the type of help that the client needs
Encourage effective coping	• Build rapport
	• Encourage recognition of resources and coping strategies that the client can draw on
	• Support the client to identify actions that they can take
Recovery or **R**eferral	• Assess the client's ability to function safely
	• With their permission, pass on information and/or signpost to other agencies, for example, counselling services
	• Identify with the client additional networks for support – friends, community or religious groups, support groups

Source: Adapted from Everly (2001).

Crisis intervention focuses on the 'positive potential of crisis' (Thompson, 2011b: 108). Such an approach enables the formulation of goals and actions that support victims of hate crime to move on and see the capacity of their own resources to effect change. Crisis intervention is a useful approach to hate crime casework support – it responds to immediacy, is time-limited (although support can continue where required) and discovers with and empowers the client to use their own resources. Crisis intervention techniques can be connected to other approaches when helping people who are in crisis and unable to cope, for example, advocating on behalf of a client.

Advocacy

Advocacy is an important skill in hate crime casework practice and support. It links to working from the victim's perspective and the core principles of hate crime casework. Advocacy is the practice of representing, under instruction from the client, 'the interests of powerless clients to powerful individuals and social structures' (Payne, 1998: 276). It can be used by a practitioner on behalf of their client, both within their own organisation and with other agencies, 'to argue for resources, or change the interpretation which powerful groups make of clients' (Payne, 1998: 276). Representation of a client can involve:

- supporting clients to represent themselves;
- arguing clients' views and needs;
- interpreting or representing the views, needs, concerns and interests of clients to others; and
- developing appropriate skills, for example, listening skills, empathy, negotiating and assertiveness skills (see Trevithick, 2012: 267).

The caseworker may use their power and influence in the interest of the real and expressed wishes of the client. Caseworkers frequently undertake advocacy activities for clients to ensure that other agencies meet their responsibilities. There are at least six principles for advocacy (Seden, 2000):

- act in the client's best interest;
- act in accordance with the client's wishes and instructions;
- keep the client properly informed;
- carry out instructions with diligence and competence;
- act impartially and offer frank, independent advice; and
- maintain rules of confidentiality.

To be a successful advocate, the practitioner will need to listen carefully, be skilled in using questions, be able to respond accurately and clearly, and be aware of non-verbal aspects of communication. An advocate will have to come up against powerful institutions (eg the police) and will need to be confident and knowledgeable about the law, the minimum service standards that a client should receive from a service and the policy and practices of other agencies, as well as able to challenge injustice where it is highlighted.

Fook (2016) helpfully distinguishes between outcome and process aspects of advocacy. The outcome of advocacy is to ensure rights and entitlements for clients but the process itself should also be an empowering experience for them. An advocate drawing on crisis intervention will act as an advocate in the early stages but support the client to develop self-advocacy, namely, to speak for themselves to protect their rights and to advance their own interests (Thompson, 2011b; Trevithick, 2012). Advocacy may result in new partnerships with, and change in practice in, other agencies.

Caseworkers cannot assume that they know best for their clients. An effective advocate will:

- ensure clients participate in their own empowerment;
- break down the actions to be taken into different aspects so that a client can see how their contributions are involved in the process; and

- be aware of their power and not be involved in 'othering' the people that they are advocating for (Fook, 2016: 192).

Advocacy is therefore closely tied to working towards and achieving both a solution and empowerment through a co-produced relationship with the client. Strengths-based approaches focus on the positive aspects and resources of a client and complement crisis intervention and advocacy in hate crime casework and support.

Strengths-based working

Strengths-based approaches concentrate on the strengths of clients in a collaborative process with a caseworker to determine outcomes that draw on the person's capabilities, support networks and motivations to meet the challenges that they are experiencing. Hate crime victims can feel disempowered by reporting agencies, disconnected from familiar networks of support and depressed and unable to participate in everyday, often taken-for-granted, activities, and may withdraw as a consequence of their experiences. As such, support providers:

> need to take the victim's specific needs as well as their social, cultural and political environment into account. To assist and support the victim's efforts in overcoming the impact of victimisation support workers will need to respect and recognise the victim's daily living environment and how this constrains or enables self-determination. (Kees et al, 2016: 32)

Strengths-based perspectives recognise the importance of resilience, namely, 'the ability of individuals to keep going in ways that enable them to overcome hazards, and to deal with risk and other forms of adversity' (Trevithick, 2012). In this respect, strengths-based approaches are able to contribute to working with clients to bring to the fore the more resilient aspects of their character in order to influence change in their circumstances (see Box 6.2).

Box 6.2: Strengths-based standards

Goal orientation

Strengths-based practice is goal oriented. The central and most crucial element of any approach is the extent to which people themselves set goals they would like to achieve in their lives.

Strengths assessment

The primary focus is not on problems or deficits. The individual is supported to recognise the resources they have that they can use to counteract any difficulty or condition.

Resources from the environment

Strengths-based practitioners believe that in every environment, there are individuals, associations, groups and institutions that have something to give that clients may find helpful. The practitioner's role may be to enable links to these resources.

Methods used for identifying client and environmental strengths for goal attainment

There are different methods for different strengths-based approaches. For example, a solution-focused approach will assist the client to set goals and focus on what they want to achieve, rather than on the problem that made them seek help. A narrative approach helps to draw out the strengths of clients from inside the problem and reframes the situation into a story of resilience by highlighting instances of strengths.

The relationship is hope-inducing

Hope can be realised through strengthened relationships with people, communities and culture.

Meaningful choice

Strengths-based perspectives recognise that the role of the caseworker is to increase and explain choices and encourage people to make their own decisions and informed choices.

Source: Adapted from Pattoni (2012).

Asking questions

A key approach in successful strengths-based work is asking quality questions that are able to identify strengths from the problems and the reality that clients are facing. Strengths will vary from person to person and it is through asking meaningful questions that solutions will be constructed. Whilst Chapter Seven discusses the types of questions a caseworker can utilise, Trevithick (2012: 350) suggests a series of questions that can be both supportive and contribute to co-producing solutions with the client, including:

- *Survival questions*: How have you managed to keep going?
- *Support questions*: Which people have given you special understanding, support and guidance? Where did you find these people?
- *Exception questions*: What was happening when things went well and what was different at that time?
- *Possibility questions*: What vision, hope and aspirations do you have for the future?
- *Esteem questions*: What are you proud of? What makes you feel good?
- *Perspective questions*: What sense do you make of what has happened? What ideas and thoughts do you have about your situation?
- *Change questions*: What would you like to change? How can I help?
- *Meaning questions*: What gives your life meaning? What do you value most?

Summary

There are various theoretical models for casework practice. This chapter has identified crisis intervention, advocacy and strengths-based perspectives as core models that can be used independently or in combination. All the approaches focus on the client's interpretation of events and validating the meaning that they give to experiences. The approaches are therefore consistent with anti-discriminatory practice, diversity and intersectionality, and empowerment. They all require excellent interpersonal and communication skills, which is the focus of Chapter Seven.

7
COMMUNICATION AND INTERPERSONAL SKILLS

Effective communication and interpersonal skills are important to understanding and achieving the victim's perspective and promoting the values and principles of hate crime casework and support. Such skills are demonstrated in interactions with a client through valuing the person and story (by believing, listening and giving time) and letting the client know that they have been understood in the casework interaction (by reflecting, paraphrasing and summarising). Confident and appropriate use of interpersonal skills forms and sustains helping relationships. Practitioners will spend a large amount of time communicating with victims, advocates, agencies, local political leaders and potentially the media.

Casework practice involves working with a range of people, all whom have different positions of power and authority. A practitioner has to be an effective communicator and draw on the skills used in everyday interactions. However, the key difference between everyday and practitioner interactions is that within the latter, the focus is on professional communication, which has a deliberate strategy that focuses the practitioner on being aware of their purpose and ensuring that the use of communication skills supports the achievement of that purpose (Healy, 2012: 22).

Communication as learned behaviour

Interpersonal and communication skills include listening, non-verbal communication, observation and verbal and counselling skills (Neville, 2009: 5–6; Healy, 2012: 22). Communication is learnt behaviour (Allen and Langford, 2008) and, as such, can often be taken for granted and go unexamined (Koprowska, 2014: 3) in relation to effectiveness or biases. Given the diversity of people who may report a hate crime, being open and aware of our own communication biases and how and when we need to adapt to respond to difference and diversity is important to building a transformative relationship.

The cultural theorist Bourdieu uses the term 'habitus' to describe taken-for-granted aspects of our culture, including our ways of thinking, feeling and communicating (Thompson, 2003: 21–2, cited in Koprowska, 2014: 4). We become aware of our habitus in our interactions with people who have a different habitus. This is crucial to a caseworker increasing their self-awareness and responding to unexpected situations where our communication skills need to adapt or respond. The caseworker cannot take communication for granted and may need to learn new ways to both express themselves and listen to others unfamiliar to them. Koprowska (2014) offers a helpful strategy in thinking about communication in terms of first- and second-order skills:

- *First-order skills* are those required in direct communication itself with service users, colleagues and others.
- *Second-order skills* are those employed in planning our communication strategy, thinking about what we are doing, observing interactions, paying attention to feedback, reviewing what has happened and modifying our next and future communications accordingly.

This is a useful distinction in practice. It enables the practitioner to distinguish between professional communications skills (eg listening, non-verbal and verbal communication, questioning) that are used in casework interactions and the need for a practitioner to be reflective and proactive about their practice-in-action.

Core communication skills

Successful communication requires self-awareness, awareness of and sensitivity towards others, and a demonstrable commitment to the values of social justice (eg equality, fairness, recognition of differences). Box 7.1 highlights the range and scope of interpersonal skills identified by helping professionals. Focusing on, for example, the value of unconditional positive regard (Rogers, 1957) would enable a caseworker to consider how to be self-aware and sensitive to the needs of others. However, more importantly, it also reminds the caseworker that 'to understand another person, and their world of meaning, we need to start by acknowledging our ignorance of that person and their social world. This involves learning to ask good questions, in ways likely to provide information that is both relevant and sufficiently detailed and to watch for clues…with being able to acknowledge the uncertainty that is inherent in looking across into another person's world' (Trevithick, 2012: 154).

'*Uncertainty*' requires the practitioner to consider their own position, power and range of identities that they may be taking for granted but could impact on the helping relationship. We cannot escape communicating ourselves to others and a practitioner engaging with hate crime clients will need to simultaneously build trust, listen, ask questions and offer reassurance and empathy, which contribute to both gathering relevant information and developing a trusting and honest relationship.

Box 7.1: Identified interpersonal skills in the helping professions

Abilities
- Leadership
- Assertiveness
- Advocacy
- Challenging
- Influencing
- Negotiating

Communication skills
- Listening
- Questioning
- Empathy
- Facilitation
- Non-verbal

Working with others
- Presenting and giving information to clients/others
- Goal setting
- Partnership working
- Awareness of others
- Interviewing skills

Values
- Helping
- Trust
- Confidentiality
- Unconditional positive regard
- Awareness of self
- Reflective practice

Source: Adapted from Neville (2009).

Listening skills

Listening to hate crime victims requires a dual strategy of hearing and understanding the message that is being conveyed (Lemos&Crane, 2004a), as well as subtly directing the client to particular questions or topics that contribute to fact finding and creating an action plan. Trevithick (2000: 57) recognises a number of different reasons why we listen to others:

- to acquire information;
- to empathise;
- to appreciate; and
- to save time by listening carefully.

By focusing on these approaches to listening, Trevithick (2012: 171) suggests that the benefits for practitioners include:

- beginning to understand the hopes, fears and expectations, and ongoing concerns that a person is harbouring;
- gaining an impression of a person's strengths and areas of vulnerability and fragility;
- understanding the meaning attached to certain experiences and events, and their ongoing impact; and
- identifying what is not being said, and to hypothesise why this might be the case.

These are all relevant benefits for a hate crime practitioner when working from a victim's perspective and will include the ability to recognise and deal with barriers that prevent listening with full attention.

Barriers to listening

Listening effectively, or active listening, requires the practitioner to be aware of possible barriers that could impede 'alertness on the part of the listener' (Lishman, 1994: 63, quoted in Trevithick, 2000: 57). Some barriers to active listening may include (Dixon and O'Hara, no date):

- forming a judgement or evaluation before we understand what is being said, or 'jumping to a conclusion';
- hearing what we want to hear;
- tuning out a point of view that differs from our own;
- formulating and rehearsing our response;
- being inattentive – thinking about something else;
- having a closed mind – you do not want to hear what the person has to say;
- feeling anxious or self-conscious;
- judging the person, either positively or negatively;
- subjective biases;

- cultural issues, for example, feeling uncomfortable with someone of the opposite sex or other people present in the room;
- external noise; and
- interruptions.

A self-reflexive and practice-in-action hate crime caseworker will want to assess each casework intervention on its own merits, putting to one side their own expertise of cases, focusing on the uniqueness of each client and listening with a freshness which demonstrates that the client is being heard.

Types of listening

The literature on interpersonal and communication skills describes a range of types of positive and negative listening (see, eg, Lishman, 2009; Egan, 2014). However, Trevithick (2012: 172) helpfully highlights three listening approaches that can benefit developing a relationship between a practitioner and client:

- *Active listening* describes a special and demanding alertness on the part of the listener, where the aim is to listen closely to the details of what is being conveyed and to ensure that the person is aware that this is happening.
- *Credulous listening* is believing what is being communicated. This description fits hate crime caseworkers who may later find information that contradicts what has been said or what they believed but are able to review their judgements in the light of new information.
- *Non-selective listening*, also known as non-directive listening, is 'listening with the third ear'. Listening using this approach focuses on what people say, how they say it, at what point they say certain things, what themes recur and also what does not get said. The intention of this approach is to minimise our own personal bias and assumptions and to follow the speaker's lead.

Empathetic listening

To the preceding list we can add *empathetic listening*, which refers to the practitioner accurately understanding what the client is feeling and thinking, as communicated and demonstrated in their non-verbal behaviour, verbal tone and expression (Healy, 2012). Rogers (1980: 137) viewed empathetic listening as an 'unappreciated' approach to 'deep listening':

> It means entering the private perceptual world of the other and becoming thoroughly at home in it. It involves being sensitive, moment by moment, to the changing felt meanings which flow in this other person, to the fear or rage or tenderness or confusion or whatever that he or she is experiencing. It means temporarily living in the other's life, moving about in it delicately without making judgments. (Rogers, 1980: 142)

To focus on and with the client is also to centre the victim's perspective, and listening with purpose enables this to be achieved. To listen purposefully, the practitioner will need to (Lemos&Crane, 2004a; Trevithick, 2012):

- minimise distractions and interruptions to the interaction;
- approach the client with an open mind;
- encourage the client to express themselves;
- give clear verbal and non-verbal signals that they have heard what is being said; and
- ask open and focused questions that identify what is important to the client and help to formulate an action plan.

Listening is a learnt skill and not an innate achievement. It requires practice, self-reflection and an awareness of one's own limits and the needs and circumstances of others, alongside recognising that there may be training needs. Essentially, listening to those who have been disempowered, had their identities threatened and undermined, or have been silenced requires a caseworker's full attention and humility and involves a range of communication skills, including non-verbal behaviour.

Evidencing listening

Paraphrasing

Paraphrasing is an important tactic to show that we have grasped and understood what is being communicated. It involves repeating back to the client a mixture of their and our words. To avoid offending or undermining the client, it is important not to change the meaning of what has been said, but to state that the practitioner is aiming to be clear about what is being told to them.

Clarifying

Clarifying evidences that the practitioner is listening, sorting out any misunderstandings and recognising the importance of what is being said. Clarifying enables a practitioner to order what may be most important for a client in developing an action plan and moving forward.

Summarising

As a tactic, summarising can be used for a range of purposes. It can be used to bring an interview to a close or to begin a follow-on interview with key points that have been raised and discussed. This process will also enable the client to view the issue from a different perspective or clarify their own thoughts. A summary partway through an interview can focus the attention of the client if the discussion has lost direction. In this way, it is a tactic that contributes to the practitioner keeping the goal of the interaction on track.

Non-verbal communication

Rogers (1957) identified three components for a successful helping relationship: empathy, congruence and unconditional positive regard (non-judgement). These can be demonstrated by a practitioner through non-verbal communication. This involves physical presence and behaviour (Healy, 2012). Non-verbal behaviour includes facial expressions, eye contact, body language and pitch and tone of voice, and can convey feelings or attitudes and symbolic communication (Lishman, 2009).

Research studies have shown that non-verbal communication can account for up to 93% of all communication (Mehrabian, 1972; Harms, 2007). A client wants to be believed and listened to, and for the caseworker to show unconditional positive regard. If a practitioner's non-verbal behaviour is negative and not in tune with their verbal communication, which may be positive, the dominant message that the client takes away is that they are not being perceived seriously or believed. Congruence is unlikely to be achieved because the non-verbal messages are:

> often the best indicators of an individual's true attitudes
> or intentions, irrespective of what has been said ... unlike
> spoken language, which is used as often to conceal thought
> as it is to express thought and which people largely control
> for their own purposes, much non-verbal language seems
> impossible to control. (Robinson, 1998: 102)

Practitioners need to be aware of their non-verbal behaviours that may be viewed as negative by clients. A model of non-verbal communication that can be used by hate crime practitioners is 'SOLER'. Developed by Egan (2014), 'SOLER' is an acronym that means:

S: *Sitting squarely* – face the client we are communicating with. This may have to be changed based on cultural norms.

O: *Open body posture* – this communicates openness and availability to the client. This involves avoiding crossing arms across the body or placing an object across one's body.

L: *Leaning towards the other* – this demonstrates interest and engagement in the client's experiences. This non-verbal cue has to respect distance so that the client does not feel uncomfortable.

E: *Eye contact* – maintain an appropriate level of eye contact to show that the client is being listened to and the practitioner is engaged with their experiences.

R: *Relaxed* – appearing relaxed in body posture and facial expression, and not looking distracted or fidgeting, will contribute to putting clients at ease.

SOLER is a useful and easy to recall model that practitioners can adapt in practice. However, hate crime practitioners will be working with a broad range of clients and will need to be aware of cultural differences and norms in their non-verbal interactions, which also focus on symbolic communication, interpersonal distance, active silence and body language.

Symbolic communication

Symbolic communication or welcoming skills include, for example, the layout, cleanliness and comfort of a reception or waiting area. The general look and feel of an interview area will hold a symbolic value with clients regarding how they will be treated. For example, is it a private and confidential space, located in an area where interruptions and disruptions can be avoided (Trevithick, 2012)? Does the reception area reflect the diversity of the client base and offer relevant information and resources? How practitioners dress will convey a message to the client of professionalism, respecting authority and respecting cultural norms in the different situations in which the client and practitioner may interact. While there are no fixed rules, recognising the symbolic importance of dress and being sensitive as a practitioner to how they will be perceived by different individuals and agencies is important

(Lishman, 2009). Finally, symbolic communication is concerned with punctuality and reliability. Showing concern is evidenced through the caseworker keeping appointments, being on time, doing what they say when they say and having proper recording equipment for the interviews, demonstrating that the practitioner is prepared and has the skills to help.

Interpersonal distance

Distance between a client and practitioner will depend on a variety of factors, including gender, disability, religion, culture and ethnicity, fear and suspicion, and the reality of the room where the interaction will take place. A practitioner who is unfamiliar with the accepted protocols or rules governing interpersonal distance in relation to gender, diversity and culture is advised to 'err on the side of caution by maintaining a polite and respectful distance' (Healy, 2012: 31). This could apply with all interactions and a practitioner can be guided by a client as to how they want to respond to interpersonal distance. For example, it is common in Western cultures to shake hands but it may not be appropriate with all clients. Some female Muslim clients may decline a handshake and some disabled clients may not be able to, which a practitioner may not be aware of until the first meeting. Politely introducing yourself and your organisation and asking them to introduce themselves will help alleviate any uncomfortableness.

Active silence

When people are talking, they should be allowed to take their time. The interviewer should be prepared for silence and not be put off by it. Silence occurs for a variety of reasons, for example, it gives space for the client to reflect on something that has been asked or a response that they have made, it could be due to something that they do not understand, or they could be waiting for a response from the practitioner. The focus on the client through these silences will convey to them that the practitioner is engaged and interested in them. If the silence is prolonged, paraphrase what was asked or talked about before the silence and ask if they have any more to say on it.

Body language

Body language includes eye contact, facial expressions, tone and volume of voice, and body position and gestures, and can have an impact on how a relationship develops between a client and practitioner. Expressing empathy and congruence can be demonstrated through the use of body language. For example, are the words and the non-verbal communication of a practitioner congruent with each other (Koprowska, 2014).

The level of eye contact cannot be specified and it varies by culture and gender. For example, too much eye contact may be seen as obtrusive or intimidating; too little eye contact may be seen as the practitioner being uninterested and not listening. Lemos&Crane (2004a) ask some self-reflexive questions, for example: 'Do I lower my eyes when I am feeling doubtful, uncertain or negative?'; 'Do I look a person directly in the eye when I am talking to them?'; and 'Do I stare?'. Knowing our own behaviours will contribute to how we respond to the needs of others from their perspective.

Facial expressions are interpreted as conveying attitudes (Lishman, 2009). Like other forms of non-verbal expression, it is important that a practitioner is aware of the nature and impact of facial expressions (Healy, 2012). Facial expressions have to be responsive to the narrative that is being given and not remain unchanging. Questions that a practitioner may ask themselves are, for example: 'Do I smile at inappropriate moments out of anxiety?'; 'Do I look unfriendly when trying to be serious?'; 'Do I look bored?'; and 'Do I nod or make a sound of acknowledgement?'. Body movements, for example, a nodding of the head, fidgeting, leaning forwards and moving arms and feet, can influence the responsiveness of a practitioner (Lishman, 2009).

The practitioner has to create a balance that indicates to the client that they are being responded to. Limited or no body movement may convey a lack of responsiveness, but excessive movement may be distracting. Mimicking the movement of the client can be a useful strategy to demonstrate that a client is being listened to. Crucially, the practitioner has to reflect on how their body language may be viewed by someone who has been abused, threatened or otherwise hurt. Is the body language open, empathetic and honest to engage with, and does it put at ease an anxious and worried client?

Observation skills

Observation is a means by which we gather information of what we see and experience in both our direct interactions and non-verbal communication (Healy, 2012; Trevithick, 2012). Healy (2012) recognises that observations provide a practitioner with at least the following:

- information about the emotional state of the client;
- a common understanding of the client's circumstances by sharing observations;
- cross-cultural learning of norms about interaction; and
- critical reflections to improve practice.

Observing the circumstances and situation of a client contributes to asking questions that enable a deeper understanding of the needs and experiences of the client.

Asking questions

The practitioner will want to gather information from a client and will ask a series of questions through the interaction to establish an agreed course of action. The quality and range of questions asked is key to the extent and type of information gathered. Questions should be asked one at a time, without asking multiple questions. Clarity of purpose and the range of interpersonal skills discussed will enable this process.

The types of questions we ask will determine the information we gather. There are broadly three types of questions (for detailed discussions, see Lishman, 2009; Trevithick, 2012; Koprowska, 2014):

- closed questions;
- open questions; and
- inner-person questions.

Closed questions

Closed questions require simple 'yes' or 'no' responses or ask for basic information that establishes facts, for example, regarding home address, diversity monitoring or where the incident occurred. Closed questions can be helpful in working with people who are lacking confidence or find it difficult to articulate their experiences. For example, a question like 'Did it hurt?' can be followed by 'How?' or 'Where?'.

Open questions

Open questions encourage the client to offer their story or explore what happened. The client is able to choose how to respond. Open questions are key to establishing the details of the complaint and how a practitioner can help. Open questions suggest the subject matter for an answer and do not presuppose what the answer may be, for example, 'Can you tell me as much as you can remember about what happened to you?' or 'How did you feel when he shouted that at you?'.

Open questions allow the practitioner to explore and ask additional questions for clarification. However, open questions may be difficult for some clients who do not find it easy to formulate their thoughts and feelings (Trevithick, 2012). In these circumstances, a combination of closed and open questions could be asked that puts the person at ease and enables a relationship to build up.

Inner-person questions

Koprowska (2014) defines inner-person questions as moving beyond factual and expansive answers in order to gather the feelings of clients. Hate crime is often an emotive experience that attacks the identity of the victim. Inner-person questions can be both open and closed, and provide information on the client's emotional and mental state, and well-being.

Additional questions

Probing and prompts

An interview that is primarily focused on open questions may need to ask follow-up questions. Probing what a client has said will enable them to give more specific information in order to confirm the practitioner's understanding of a situation and to gain clarification, for example, 'Is this the first time that this has happened?'. Prompts are used to nudge the client to provide further information, for example, 'Have you reported this to the police, local anti-social behaviour officer or law centre?'.

Leading and loaded questions

Leading questions indicate the answer that the practitioner wants to hear and coerce the other person into agreement (Koprowska, 2014), for example, 'So the police are to blame?'. Loaded questions contain value judgements that undermine the practitioner's values of empathy and empowerment because they may imply disbelief, suspicion or even aggression (Lemos&Crane, 2004b), for example, 'Are you sure it is a hate crime?'.

Helping and valuing the client

Helping is an interaction with people who are often disempowered and discriminated, whose lives have often been made insecure, and who may never have spoken about their experiences. Demonstrating empathy and genuineness in a casework interaction requires an acceptance of both the realities of everyday hate crime and the need to enter into the life of the client without judgement.

Interpersonal skills are needed to form and sustain helping relationships. In hate crime casework, this may be a short interaction or a lengthy process. The casework relationship is a form of helping that encompasses demonstrating that the client has been valued, through listening and giving them time, and that clients know that they have being understood, which caseworkers can demonstrate by reflecting, paraphrasing and summarising the interaction (Neville, 2009). In a helping relationship, caseworkers have to be aware of and respond from a non-judgemental approach in their communication with clients (see Box 7.2).

Box 7.2: Identified attributes of a non-judgemental approach

- Being open minded and accepting clients exactly as they are.
- Accepting clients' accounts, their versions of their experience of hate violence and their subsequent decisions.
- Not evaluating clients' behaviour, decisions or actions.
- Accepting clients' decisions and not making decisions for them.
- Allowing clients to act on their own decisions.
- Not pushing the caseworker's own ideas and thoughts about how to move forward onto clients.
- Being careful and cautious with recommendations and advice.

Source: Kees et al (2016).

Summary

Communication and interpersonal skills cannot be taken for granted. They are learned behaviours and caseworkers may need to reflect on their own approach to effective listening, observing and what their non-verbal cues may be communicating to the client. Listening is a key skill in hate crime casework and support. It is from being listened to that a client feels believed and validated. Similarly, asking appropriate and quality questions that elicit relevant information from the client will contribute to creating action plans. Communication and interpersonal skills have to be practised and it is in their interaction with clients, usually in an interview, or through fact-finding that this occurs. The fact-finding process is explored in Chapter Eight.

FACT FINDING

Fact finding with a client has a critical impact on their perception of the service, the support that they are likely to receive, their ability to make decisions, what they consider to be in their best interests and whether they cooperate in any legal action that may follow. It also impacts on how trust and relations between local communities and support/investigating agencies develop. This chapter focuses on the key approaches for effective interviewing for fact finding.

It is important to recognise that we are always communicating, and in the interview process, the caseworker will be communicating to the client their belief in the client, their service standards and their professional expectations. We communicate both verbally and non-verbally with our clients. Making people feel at ease and welcome is as important as effective listening and responding. Effective listening means making sure that the client knows that they have been heard, that their views have been respected and, where possible, that their views will be responded to. A busy caseworker will need to ensure that they have appropriate time and find a safe environment where effective communication can take place.

The initial interview

The initial or first interview is crucial to building a relationship, building trust in the process and enabling the victim to articulate what they believe has happened to them without judgement, fear or recrimination. The first interview is an essential part of the advocacy and empowerment process. The key objectives of the first interview are to:

- reassure and empathise with the victim;
- untangle the facts from their experiences;
- explore the various options and choices that the victim has;
- support the victim to make reasonable decisions that ensure their safety and security; and
- co-produce an action plan that is understood and agreed.

The progress of the first interview can be somewhat less than linear. Victims may not follow a pattern or script of question answering. Clients may vent and be emotional, angry and even confused when telling and often retelling their story. The caseworker has to provide a safe and open environment and be empathetic in their response. Clients have the right to talk about and show their feelings about the circumstances that they are in and the caseworker should actively encourage these feelings as part of casework practice to move towards co-developing solutions and actions. The client may tell their experiences without an order or sequence. The caseworker has to be prepared for these responses and treat and respond to each case as unique. This may be the first time that the client has had a chance to tell anyone what has been going on and to share their problems with someone who is supportive and prepared to listen without judgement.

Key stages of the interview

There are different stages to an interview (Lemos&Crane, 2004b) that can have the effect of both reassuring the client, gathering information and enabling the interview to achieve its key objectives. These stages have been adapted and extended.

Agreeing the location

When and where a first interview or meeting with the client is held will depend on a number of issues, including access, confidentiality, their own circumstances, who they reported to and when and where they themselves may feel comfortable to meet and talk about their experiences. If a hate crime has taken place in the home, for example, a third space may need to be found. From the caseworker perspective, the logistics of safety, travel, time and their role within hate crime support (eg a dedicated support worker will be able to make a home visit but a Citizens Advice Bureau advisor will not) will be key factors in determining the location of the first interview/meeting. It would also be important to establish if children will be present in the interview (either at an office or home), and toys may be provided in the office.

Introductions

The interview process should start with the caseworker introducing themselves and anyone who is with them, such as an interpreter, a colleague or other agency representative. Other people who are present in the room, such as relatives and friends of the victim, should also be asked to introduce themselves. Caseworkers must carry photographic identification to ensure legitimacy and professionalism. Interviewing someone in their home may result in different distractions, for example, noise, interruptions and children entering or leaving the room. The caseworker will have to manage these and other possible distractions in a sensitive and appropriate manner, for example, asking politely for the television/radio/music to be turned off or setting some ground rules with children who may get upset if they are in the same room where the interview is being held. However, this is as much a matter for the parents and children as the caseworker.

Confidentiality and informed consent

Establishing ground rules also includes explaining confidentiality, anonymity and gaining informed consent from the client. The caseworker cannot guarantee not to discuss the case with anybody else, but this may be possible to anonymise. Further, if the client wants to make a formal complaint against a perpetrator (if they have not already done so) after this first interview, confidentiality will be severely limited. If the alleged perpetrators are known and, for example, live in the local area, an assurance will need to be made that information will not be disclosed without the explicit consent of the client, even if the perpetrator asks.

Informed consent is paramount. It is important that the client, who may be upset and confused, understands the process of the interview and the information that they are providing. Informed consent involves the caseworker using clear and understandable language to inform clients of: the purpose of the interview; what will happen next; the clients' right to refuse or withdraw consent, as well as the time frame covered by the consent; and their opportunity to ask questions (Hepworth et al, 2010: 65).

Informed consent is not merely a formality to go through at the early stages of an interview, but an ongoing process. As the case develops and information is given and advice and actions are taken, informed consent may need to be revisited (Hepworth et al, 2010: 65). Informed consent involves the client agreeing that they fully understand what will happen and feel comfortable to sign a form that clearly states what they have agreed to. A copy of the consent form should be given to the client. Informed consent protects the caseworker in relation to boundaries, expectations and realistic options for action.

Explaining your role and procedures

Caseworkers essentially come in many guises, for example, dedicated hate crime officers, social housing anti-social behaviour officers, police officers, teachers and community development workers. Each caseworker operates from their organisational practice and within the limitations of the service they provide, and will have different roles and responsibilities. For example, while a dedicated hate crime officer will advocate solely on behalf of a client, a police or anti-social behaviour officer will have to potentially investigate and hear the views of the alleged perpetrators and respond accordingly.

To provide confidence and reassurance, the caseworker and the interview can be used to communicate the essential aspects of the service's hate crime policy and/or approach. Places for People, for example, clearly state in their community safety policy and procedure that after a complaint of hate crime has been made, they will, among other actions, 'Maintain regular contact with witnesses to keep them up to date with the action we are taking and provide tailored support to witnesses as necessary' (Place for People, 2015).

The key factors to be communicated to the client will vary by organisation. For example, a housing-based service should communicate that: the organisational policy or service approach is to aim to stop the hate violence and crime; both practical and emotional support will be provided; if the problem continues and is classified as a hate crime, legal action will be considered or taken in partnership with other organisations; and any actions taken will be in their best interests and communicated to them.

Establish what happened

The interview is a process of listening, gathering information, building confidence and reassuring the client. It will enable the interaction if an open question is asked, such as, 'In your own words, describe what has happened in as much detail as possible'. The skills of the caseworker will also need to untangle what may be an unstructured narrative in detail from the client. This may be the first time that the client has talked in great detail of what has happened with someone who is supportive and has the time to listen. However, a caseworker's time is limited and a scheduled amount of time must be agreed in advance.

At this stage, the caseworker will be focused on identifying information and providing responses that achieve the five key objectives of the first interview. Managing this exchange will work better if a client is able to vent and is reassured that what they are feeling is taken seriously. Taking detailed notes may not be possible at this stage, but enough can be taken to establish what happened, where and when, who was responsible, whether there were any witnesses, whether they have any supportive networks, what the impacts have been, and whether there are any children or vulnerable people at risk. Each of these key pieces of information should be taken in turn. All information that is noted should also aim to establish a timeline and be written up as soon as possible after the interview.

Reassurance and safety

Many incidents of hate crime occur in and around the home and can leave people feeling vulnerable and in fear. Other incidents occur on the streets, in specific locations and in public places. Wherever the incident has occurred, the caseworker has to make the client feel safe and reassured throughout the interview. Considering the safety of the client and other affected people is crucial.

As the narrative of the interview unfolds, the caseworker will be able to co-produce immediate actions, for example, emergency repairs to the home, reporting to the police or medical treatment. Knowing the housing tenure of the client becomes crucial because a social housing provider will have a hate crime policy and procedure and will offer additional support and help. Knowing if the client has support from family and friends who may be able to help will also be useful. Hate crime victims have often told people they know what is happening to them. However, in some cases, family members may be the perpetrators and the client could be isolated from such informal support. A client must know other services that are available in the area to support a client and be able to provide this information. Family and friends are an additional resource to reassure the client that they may be able to help; visiting the client, leaving their home together, going to the shops or taking children to school will reassure, increase feelings of safety and reduce isolation.

Perpetrators may be known to the client and the caseworker will want to discuss what options and actions are available. Only after a client feels secure and safe should the caseworker talk about steps that could be taken against an alleged perpetrator. Lemos&Crane (2004b: 4) suggest the following helpful strategy:

> They should establish whether the perpetrator was seen and, if so, identified. Sometimes people experiencing harassment will say that the perpetrators are not known to them, when they may be. They are keen to avoid reprisals and, therefore, they think it is wiser 'not to rock the boat' by naming them. The interviewer should emphasise that action will only be taken against the perpetrators if the person who has been harassed agrees it is in their best interests.

A client may not feel that it is safe for them to return home or to another location. The caseworker will have to make decisions with the client as to what can happen next to assure their safety. For example, a client suffering threats or actual violence in the home may not want to go back and will require an immediate response from the caseworker and others, which includes:

- advising the victim to seek immediate medical attention;
- taking photographic evidence;
- discussing whether the police should be informed and how they can help;
- contacting relevant services and agencies who can offer support; and
- if emergency accommodation is not available, offering support in locating friends or other family members with whom the client will feel and be safe.

Co-producing options with the client

Working with the client to develop and communicate options can take time and also depends on the immediacy of the situation. Options will be revealed through the interview and how the narrative unfolds. The caseworker should agree with the client what they are going to do from the information that they have gathered. Including the client in the planning gives them back ownership, control, power and influence over the outcome, which is often stripped away after being a victim of hate crime. Options cannot be pre-judged:

> The main aim of the first interview is empowerment. The interviewer's job is to generate options so the person who has been harassed can choose what the next steps should be. The interviewer should not tell them what they think is best for them, or what they want is impossible. (Lemos&Crane, 2004b: 3)

Caseworkers should not promise what they cannot deliver. For example, saying that the perpetrator will be prosecuted or moved (if a social housing tenant) will potentially raise unrealistic expectations and may undermine the caseworker–client relationship. Listening to the actions that a client wants and the caseworker making suggestions will generate a list of options that will enable the client to make informed and empowered decisions. The caseworker must be assured that the client fully understands:

- what the options are;
- the chances of succeeding;
- the timescales involved; and
- the likely consequences (Commission for Racial Equality, 2000).

Options may also include signposting to other services who may be able to provide additional advice and emotional or practical support. The role of a caseworker from any agency is to be able to offer advice of where else a client can go for help, advice and assistance. These may include:

- the police;
- housing provider;
- schools and other educational establishments;
- anti-social behaviour unit/officer;
- Citizens' Advice Bureaux;
- law centres;
- victim support schemes;
- local counselling service;
- local community and faith groups; and
- national reporting centres (eg Tell MAMA, Stop Hate UK, True Vision).

Knowing what such agencies can offer if signposted to them will enable a client to make informed decisions. Caseworkers may want to keep a directory of local and national services as part of a victim support pack that can be given to a client.

Preparing and agreeing an action plan

The various options discussed in the interview should lead to creating an action plan that is agreed with and understood by the client. From the perspective of a caseworker, the action plan may be known as a case management action plan, which provides the client with an individualised, personalised plan for their support and agreed actions that can be reviewed.

The action plan will be organised around identified priorities arising from the interview. Box 8.1 identifies that these actions can be organised as immediate/emergency, urgent, medium-term and long-term actions (Commission for Racial Equality, 2000), but the boundaries will be fluid depending on the circumstances of the case. Immediate action has to be taken particularly if the client is vulnerable and/or feels at risk of further attacks. Urgent action may involve situations that include identified actions in the policies and procedures of organisations. Medium-term responses may include the client approaching other agencies for support and advocacy or a service instigating actions against a perpetrator. Longer-term responses are appropriate in situations where the agreed action taken by different agencies has not resolved the problem, which is ongoing.

Box 8.1: Priorities for action

Immediate/emergency
- Medical treatment
- Emergency intervention and referral to other agencies
- Repairs to damaged property to secure it
- Move to safe accommodation
- Financial assistance
- Security presence to reassure

Urgent
- Removal of graffiti
- Contact friends and family
- Install additional security
- Provide a 24-hour helpline
- True Vision reporting pack
- Advocacy

Medium term
- Signposting to other agencies
- Access to specialist legal advice

Longer term
- Moving home
- Leaving the area
- Preparing a legal case

Hate crime is reported because victims want the problem to stop or it has got serious (Chahal and Julienne, 1999; Chakraborti et al, 2014); they rarely want revenge or punishment (Lemos&Crane, 2004b). The interview is an opportunity to identify and gather facts from the client, and to reassure and work with them to create a series of actions that both they and the caseworker will move forward with.

Diary sheets and support packs

Towards the end of the interview, clients can be given a victim support pack and asked to complete a hate incident log or diary as incidents occur or soon after. Clients need to be encouraged to keep records or a diary of ongoing hate incidents. A simple diary can be provided that lists the date, time, nature and location of incidents, the description of the perpetrator, and the existence of any witnesses. A diary sheet can help inform and build a picture of the hate incidents and provide potential evidence for legal cases and victim personal statements.

A victim support pack includes at least the following:

- contact details of relevant agencies, including emergency services and third-party agencies;
- information on what a hate crime is and actions that can be taken to stop it;
- diary sheets;
- hate crime policy and procedures or statements;
- the service standards of the organisation and what a client can expect; and
- how to complain if the client is not satisfied with the service.

Closing the interview

It has been argued that 'the interview should end when the person who has been harassed is ready, not when the interviewer wants to, or because they feel they have gone as far as they can' (Lemos&Crane, 2004b: 6). However, time is a precious commodity and a caseworker is likely to be working on multiple cases. Often, the initial interview will be for about one hour and key information will be identified and noted, options will be discussed, and an action plan will be agreed. If a second or more detailed interview is required, or if ongoing support is needed for the client, these should be arranged as part of the action planning.

In closing this first interview, the caseworker should ensure at least the following:

- that the client has had sufficient time to tell their story and has provided all the relevant information to progress with the complaint;
- that the caseworker has nothing further to ask;
- that an action plan has been agreed and signed;
- that, if necessary, a follow-up meeting or support has been agreed;
- that if the caseworker is the 'lead agency' in the case, the client has been told what will happen next, and that any information that the client may receive from different agencies will be kept in touch with; and
- that the client knows when the caseworker will be contacting them again.

Back at the office

The caseworker should write up the case notes soon after the interview, and within a reasonable time (24–48 hours) should contact the client to summarise the interview, agreed action plans and any progress that has been made. While writing a letter/email will be a preferred method, this may not be ideal in all cases and will be agreed with the client. If relevant, the client should be reminded to log and take details of any further incidents.

Any communication with a client will take into account language and other needs to enable the client to be fully informed. The caseworker, as the lead agency, will need to communicate with other relevant agencies as agreed with the client and keep records of the case. The caseworker will keep the client informed about any progress, however small, on an agreed regular basis.

Summary

An interview with a client is a structured event that has clear objectives for both parties. For the client, the interview communicates reassurance, believing, offering support and an action plan. However, for the caseworker, the fact-finding interview provides an opportunity to understand the needs of the client, to develop a picture of what is happening and to consider which other agencies the client may want to receive help from. These interviews can be wounding; listening to the emotions and experiences of clients over a long period of time is likely to have an impact on caseworkers. Chapter Nine discusses the issues relating to self-care and reflective practice for caseworkers.

9
SELF-CARE

Hate crime casework and support offers help, assistance and advice to people who have been the victims of hate violence, repeat victimisation and, in some cases, secondary victimisation. A hate crime service is often accessed at crisis points where the coping mechanisms of the individual can no longer manage or process what they are suffering. In entering a helping service, the client is seeking support, reassurance and solutions, often from a caseworker. While the role of the caseworker is to provide support and show empathy and compassion, there are impacts on them that also need to be identified and responded to.

The helping professions can be very effective and rewarding forms of practice (Thompson, 2011b). In my work with hate crime professionals, they identified strongly with a commitment to social justice and working for the client that is often viewed as changing not only the lives of individuals and families, but also communities, agencies, institutions, and society. Helping professionals are driven by a belief in their capacity to make a difference; for a client to be helped through an ethos of genuineness and caring; and these beliefs and approaches will sustain them in working with clients with enduring difficulties (Koprowska, 2014).

I have met caseworkers who, while doing their job, are suffering from depression, are close to burnout, are feeling unsupported and isolated, are managing an increasingly large caseload and complex political relationships with other agencies, and are working on fixed-term contracts in projects with time-limited funding. Hate crime practitioners also have needs that must be recognised and responded to by the services that employ them.

Burnout and vicarious trauma

Working with the emotional and practical demands of victims of hate crime, in a pressurised political environment and with increasing workloads and expectations, can lead to burnout. Burnout is a 'state where people can no longer connect authentically to their work, to themselves or to service users' (Koprowska, 2014: 199). It has three aspects:

- emotional exhaustion;
- depersonalisation; and
- loss of personal accomplishment (Maslach et al, 1996, cited in Koprowska, 2014: 199).

Burnout can reduce a caseworker's ability to empathise, concentrate and provide an appropriate and professional response, and result in loss of satisfaction or depression. Indeed, a hate crime service that I worked with recognised burnout as a direct and inevitable consequence of the job role. They recognised that hate violence caseworkers were often burnt out within two years of working directly with clients and had a policy of 'regeneration', namely, recruiting new staff as caseworkers.

Listening to, recounting and responding to the experiences of hate violence victims can result in secondary traumatic stress or vicarious trauma. Such levels of distress require the same care and compassion from managers and supervisors that is given to clients and presented as core service standards.

Stress management and supervision

A hate crime support practitioner has to provide a professional service regardless of their own thoughts, feelings and views about a client, responses from other service providers, and, indeed, any personal problems of their own. Casework involves an interaction of emotions and the caseworker will have to put aside their own emotions to work constructively with clients and other professionals. Support and supervision are crucial for a caseworker in reducing pressure, recognising burnout and trauma, and reinforcing and boosting their own coping methods (Thompson, 2011b) in order to reduce stress. The supervision process has to benefit the caseworker, and caseworkers themselves must be asking of the service and management:

- Am I receiving support (supervision, debriefing, training and professional development) to help me do my work and cope with the pressures of it?
- Is the support sufficient? What more do I need and who can I ask?
- Do I have access to sufficient informal support (eg family or friends)?
- Do I have time for other interests outside of work?

The supervision relationship

Supervisors in helping professions should be supportive and conscious of the emotional work that caseworkers undertake and not add to the pressures that they may be under. While, in a pressurised service, compassion and understanding of the needs of staff may become a secondary issue, this will fundamentally affect the ethos and approach of the service to clients. Compassion must run through the service. A basic supervision relationship should recognise and respond to the following:

- workload management;
- demand, the intensity of casework and time commitment to cases;
- how much out-of-hours work is being done;
- training and professional development;
- release of intense feelings generated by casework;
- giving constructive feedback and appreciation;
- the needs of the caseworker to perform effectively;

- opportunities for the caseworker to benefit from peer group support; and
- reflective practice.

Reflective practice

Reflective practice is the ability to reflect on an action so as to engage in a process of continuous learning (Schon, 1983). Hate crime casework generates both an emotional and practical intensity that a caseworker and the service can always learn from and receive support about in the supervision relationship. Reflective practice is 'a commitment to examine and to think critically about the approaches we adopt in practice with a view to improving our work' (Trevithick, 2012: 98). In supervision or a peer support group, a caseworker can put themselves outside of the case and deconstruct and analyse the intervention with themselves, a supervisor or a peer group. Box 9.1 provides one method for reflective practice developed by Gibbs (1988), which focuses on a structured debriefing.

Box 9.1: Gibbs' model for reflective practice

Description
What happened? Describe the case but do not make any judgements or draw conclusions.

Feelings
What were your feelings and reactions? Describe them but do not analyse them.

Evaluation
Make value judgements of what was good or bad about the experience from your perspective.

Analysis
What sense can you make of the situation? What do you think was really going on? What were the experiences of other people?

Conclusions (general)

In a general sense, what can you conclude from these experiences and the analyses you have undertaken?

Conclusions (specific)

What can be concluded about your own specific, unique, personal situation or way of working?

Action plans

What are you going to do differently in this type of situation next time? What steps will you take on the basis of what you have learnt?

Source: Gibbs (1988).

Undertaken in a supportive environment, reflective practice can contribute to a practitioner developing personally, recognising their own inner strengths, coping mechanisms and areas for improvement and need, and updating their skills and knowledge.

Accessing external counselling

It is the responsibility of the employer to look after the well-being of an employee. Many workplaces have access to free confidential counselling helplines. However, hate crime caseworkers work in a variety of settings and some may not have such access to external support. There are sometimes free, or very reasonably priced, counselling services in many areas and these should be explored and made available.

Summary

Hate crime casework has emotional consequences for the practitioner and these should be recognised and responded to by the service provider. The service should provide a caseworker with effective and regular supervision and support that aims to look after their emotional and professional development needs. Developing approaches to reflective practice with a supervisor or a peer support group can build coping strategies in caseworkers and improve practice and learning that can be applied back into casework practice.

POSTSCRIPT

At the time of writing, we await to hear if the murder of a Polish man, Arkadiusz Jozwik, in Harlow, England, was a hate crime. In recent months, we have lived through extensive online and offline news reporting of hate incidents in various locations of the country. According to Scotland Yard's Deputy Commissioner Craig Mackey, the campaign and referendum to leave the European Union, known as 'Brexit', has 'unleashed something in people' (BBC News, 2016). This unleashing led to a sharp increase in the number of hate crimes (particularly racist and religious hate crime) in England, Wales and Northern Ireland prior to and following the referendum on membership of the European Union, which was held on 23 June 2016.

In the four days after the referendum, the National Police Chiefs' Council (NPCC) indicated a 57% rise in the reporting of hate crime compared to the same period in 2015. In the four weeks since 16 June 2016, there were 6,193 hate crimes reported to the police, with the most common offences being harassment, assault, verbal abuse and spitting. There were 3,001 hate crimes reported in the first two weeks of July 2016, namely, the weeks following the referendum result. While this was a reduction by 6% on the previous fortnight, it was still 20% higher than the same period of 2015.[1]

PostRefRacism (2016) published a report compiled by activists from three social media platforms that highlighted 645 racist and xenophobic incidents reported to them. Nearly a third of the victims were black and minority ethnic people, with 'South Asians' reporting the most incidents (16%). Eastern Europeans were the next largest group and, in particular, Polish people were targeted. Racist abuse commonly referred to telling people to 'go home', or 'we voted you out'. How did we get here and what are its implications on casework support?

The Committee on the Elimination of Racial Discrimination (CERD, 2016) reported that it was:

> Deeply concerned that the referendum campaign was marked by divisive, anti-immigrant and xenophobic rhetoric, and that many politicians and prominent political figures not only failed to condemn it, but also created and entrenched prejudices, thereby emboldening individuals to carry out acts of intimidation and hate towards ethnic or ethno-religious minority communities and people who are visibly different.

CERD (2016) further stated that it:

> Remains concerned at the negative portrayal of ethnic or ethno-religious minority communities, immigrants, asylum-seekers and refugees by the media in the State party, particularly in the aftermath of terrorist attacks, as well as the rise of racist hate speech on the Internet.

The UK government responded by stating that the UK has 'one of the strongest legislative frameworks in the world to protect communities from hostility, violence and bigotry'.[2] However, we know that there is a substantial attrition rate from hate crime reporting to prosecution, and victims of hate crime may not feel or receive justice. This can impact on the confidence of different social groups to report hate crimes.

We also know that a spike in hate crime reporting occurs after a trigger event such as 'Brexit' or a terrorist attack. Hate crime has the potential to increase in periods of uncertainty, fuelled by the negative discourse of the media and politicians. Hate crime casework and support becomes central at these points of spikes, uncertainty and failure to get the justice victims seek. Will victims receive the support, advice and assistance they need from caseworkers, who are likely to be working to capacity and few and far between?

The UK government's hate crime plan, *Action against hate* (Home Office, 2016), was published a few days after the referendum. This is a four-year plan (following on from three previous plans) and sets out the UK government's programme of action to tackle hate crime until May 2020 across England and Wales. The plan aims to work in partnership with communities and join up work across the hate crime strands to draw on and share best practice. The plan focuses on preventing and responding to hate crime, increasing the reporting of hate crime and providing improved support for victims (Home Office, 2016).

A policy of increasing reporting will mean that the numbers of hate crime victims who may need support will also increase. Minimum support for victims can only be improved if there is well-resourced casework that is empowering and victim-oriented. There are also the increasing challenges of cyber-hate and the inclusion of newly recognised forms of hate crime (Home Office, 2016: 27). Yet, the government action plan is generally silent on providing financial resource to fund hate crime casework. For victims to trust the criminal justice system and be able to access the minimum service standards that is their right, there is a need for policy and strategy that goes beyond advocating increasing reporting to providing adequate infrastructure for hate crime casework and support services. This would go some way towards recognising the realities of hate crime and the changes that caseworkers and support services make to the lives of its victims.

Notes

[1] See: http://www.independent.co.uk/news/uk/crime/post-brexit-increase-in-hate-crimes-continues-as-police-promise-crackdown-a7150901.html

[2] See: http://www.bbc.co.uk/news/uk-37193140

CURRENT UK HATE CRIME LEGISLATION

What follows are extracts from the College of Policing's (2014) *Hate crime operational guidance*, reproduced with permission from the College of Policing Ltd. Section numbers are as they appear in the guidance.

2 Legislation

Legislation has provided three specific options to assist in combating hate crime. These are:

- racially or religiously aggravated offences
- specific offences that will always be classified as a hate crime
- enhanced sentencing legislation for any offence.

Note: where a piece of legislation in this section is not applicable to Northern Ireland this is stated. In addition, see **2.3.5 The Criminal Justice (No. 2) (Northern Ireland) Order 2004** for legislation which applies in Northern Ireland only.

2.1 Racially or religiously aggravated offences

The Crime and Disorder Act 1998 (the 1998 Act) introduced racially aggravated offences. The Anti-terrorism, Crime and Security Act 2001 amended the 1998 Act to also include religiously aggravated offences.

Sections 29–32 of the 1998 Act identify a number of offences which, if motivated by hostility or where the offender demonstrates hostility, can be treated as racially or religiously aggravated. These offences can be the preferred charge where there is evidence of racial or religious aggravation when committing the offence.

The 1998 Act creates the following racially or religiously aggravated offences:

- assaults (section 29)
- criminal damage (section 30)
- public order offences (section 31)
- harassment (section 32).

For any other offence where there is evidence that it was motivated by hate, or for any other strand of hate crime, the CPS [Crown Prosecution Service] can request enhanced sentencing. For further information see **2.3.4 Enhanced sentencing for other crimes motivated by hostility**.

2.1.1 Definitions for racially or religiously aggravated offences

Section 28 of the 1998 Act defines the terms racially aggravated and religiously aggravated.

An offence is racially aggravated if:

- at the time of committing the offence, or immediately before or after doing so, the offender demonstrates towards the victim of the offence hostility based on the victim's membership (or presumed membership) of a racial group, or

- the offence is motivated (wholly or partly) by hostility towards members of a racial group based on their membership of that group.

An offence is religiously aggravated if:

- at the time of committing the offence, or immediately before or after doing so, the offender demonstrates towards the victim of the offence hostility based on the victim's membership (or presumed membership) of a religious group, or
- the offence is motivated (wholly or partly) by hostility towards members of a religious group based on their membership of that group.

A racial group means any group of people defined by reference to their race, colour, nationality (including citizenship), ethnic or national origins.

A religious group means any group of people defined by reference to religious belief or lack of religious belief.

2.1.2 Use of the term hostility

For the purpose of both racially and religiously aggravated offences, the term hostility is not defined in the legislation. However, Guidance on Disability Hate Crime states that:

> In the absence of a precise legal definition of hostility, consideration should be given to ordinary dictionary definitions, which include ill-will, ill-feeling, spite, contempt, prejudice, unfriendliness, antagonism, resentment and dislike.

2.2 Specific hate crime offences

A number of specific offences have been created by legislation which, when the relevant points have been proved, will always be considered as hate crime. They include incitement offences which are covered in **13 Inciting hatred**.

Specific hate crime offences should always be recorded as hate crimes and may be considered by the CPS when making charging decisions.

2.2.1 Incitement to racial hatred

Section 18 of the Public Order Act 1986 makes it an offence for a person to use threatening, abusive or insulting words or behaviour, or to display any written material which is threatening, abusive or insulting, intending to stir up racial hatred, or where having regard to all the circumstances racial hatred is likely to be stirred up.

2.2.2 Incitement to hatred on the grounds of religion

Section 29B of the Public Order Act 1986 makes it an offence for a person to use threatening words or behaviour, or display any written material which is threatening, with the intention to stir up religious hatred.

2.2.3 Incitement to hatred based on sexual orientation

Section 29B of the Public Order Act 1986 makes it an offence for a person to use threatening words or behaviour, or display any written material which is threatening, with the intention to stir up hatred on the grounds of sexual orientation.

Incitement offences contained in the Public Order Act 1986 also include offences of distribution, broadcasting, performance, public display and possession of inflammatory material. For further information and guidance on how to the use [sic] incitement legislation, see **13 Inciting hatred**.

2.2.4 Racialist chanting

Section 3 of the Football (Offences) Act 1991 makes it an offence to engage or take part in chanting of an indecent or racialist nature at a designated football match.

Chanting means the repeated uttering of any words or sounds, whether alone or in concert with one or more others.

Of a racialist nature means consisting of, or including, matter which is threatening, abusive or insulting to a person by reason of their colour, race, nationality (including citizenship), ethnic or national origins.

2.3 Sentencing for hate crime

Sections 145 and 146 of the Criminal Justice Act 2003 instruct the courts to enhance a sentence against an offender, and to declare in court that they are doing so.

2.3.1 Section 145 Criminal Justice Act 2003

This section requires the courts to consider racial or religious hostility as an aggravating factor when deciding on the sentence for any offence which has not been identified as a racially or religiously aggravated offence under the 1998 Act.

Section 145 – increase in sentences for racial or religious aggravation

1. This section applies where a court is considering the seriousness of an offence other than one under sections 29 to 32 of the Crime and Disorder Act 1998 (c. 37) (racially or religiously aggravated assaults, criminal damage, public order offences and harassment etc.).
2. If the offence was racially or religiously aggravated, the court –
   (a) must treat that fact as an aggravating factor, and
   (b) must state in open court that the offence was so aggravated.
3. Section 28 of the Crime and Disorder Act 1998 (meaning of racially or religiously aggravated) applies for the purposes of this

section in the same way as it applies for the purposes of sections 29 to 32 of that Act.

2.3.2 Section 146 Criminal Justice Act 2003

Section 146 addresses increased sentences for aggravation related to sexual orientation, disability or transgender identity.

1. This section applies where the court is considering the seriousness of an offence committed in any of the circumstances mentioned in subsection (2).
2. Those circumstances are –
   (a) that, at the time of committing the offence, or immediately before or after doing so, the offender demonstrated towards the victim of the offence hostility based on –
   (i) the sexual orientation (or presumed sexual orientation) of the victim, or
   (ii) a disability (or presumed disability) of the victim, or
   (iii) the victim being (or presumed to be) transgender.
   (b) that the offence is motivated (wholly or partly) –
   (i) by hostility towards persons who are of a particular sexual orientation, or
   (ii) by hostility towards persons who have a disability or a particular disability, or
   (iii) by hostility towards persons who are transgender.
3. The court –
   (a) must treat the fact that the offence was committed in any of those circumstances as an aggravating factor, and
   (b) must state in open court that the offence was committed in such circumstances.
4. It is immaterial for the purposes of paragraph (a) or (b) of subsection (2) whether or not the offender's hostility is also based, to any extent, on any other factor not mentioned in that paragraph.
5. In this section disability means any physical or mental impairment.

6. In this section references to being transgender include references to being transsexual, or undergoing, proposing to undergo or having undergone a process or part of a process of gender reassignment.

2.3.3 Definitions for sections 145 and 146

For the definition of hostility, see **2.1.2 Use of the term hostility**.

2.3.4 Enhanced sentencing for other crimes motivated by hostility

For cases where the hostility is directed towards a characteristic not covered by section 145 or 146, eg, age, gender or lifestyle choice, the courts may consider the targeted nature of the crime when calculating the seriousness of the offence under section 143 of the Criminal Justice Act 2003. The Sentencing Guidelines Council specifically includes the following among the 'factors indicating higher culpability' when calculating the seriousness of an offence:

- offence motivated by hostility towards a minority group, or a member or members of it
- deliberate targeting of vulnerable victim(s).

For further information see <u>Sentencing guidelines</u>.

2.3.5 The Criminal Justice (No. 2) (Northern Ireland) Order 2004

This Order does not create any new offences based on a hate-related motivation. It instructs the courts to increase a sentence against an offender, and to declare in court that they are doing so, when it is found that an offender demonstrated, or was motivated by, hostility based on religion, race, sexual orientation or disability.

Article 3 extends the provisions of Article 8 of the Public Order (Northern Ireland) Order 1987, which defines fear and hatred, to include sexual orientation or disability.

Under Article 8 of the Public Order (NI) Order 1987, fear and hatred is defined as follows:

- fear means the fear of a group of people defined by references to religious belief, sexual orientation, disability, colour, race, nationality (including citizenship) or ethnic or national origins
- hatred means the hatred against a group of people defined by references to religious belief, sexual orientation, disability, colour, race, nationality (including citizenship) or ethnic or national origins.

13 Inciting hatred

The Public Order Act 1986 includes specific offences of inciting hatred on the grounds of race, religion and sexual orientation.

These are relatively new offences and there is not a great deal of case law to help make decisions. All allegations of incitement to, and stirring up, hatred must be referred to the central special crime and counter-terrorism division of the CPS, and require the consent of the Attorney General to proceed to court.

Incitement offences have been the subject of considerable debate. The nature of these offences can lead to conflict between individuals and groups about the balance of freedom of expression and protection from hatred. The police have seen how the expression of a personal belief can be interpreted by others as likely to stir up hatred. Incitement can arise from one religious group's view on another's religious belief or from a religious person's view on sexual orientation or vice versa.

Whether a particular act comes within the behaviour covered by the offences is ultimately for the court to decide. The CPS has to judge in each case whether the evidence supports a reasonable prospect of a successful prosecution.

In considering the offences of inciting hatred on the basis of religion and sexual orientation, Parliament accepted evidence that legislation is necessary to prevent such activity. It took a view that the legislation contains a sufficiently high threshold, so that any interference with freedom of expression was justifiable under the terms of the European Convention on Human Rights (ECHR) and the Human Rights Act 1998.

Article 10 of the ECHR says that any interference with freedom of expression must be prescribed by law. It must also be:

- necessary in a democratic society
- in the interests of national security, territorial integrity or public safety
- for the prevention of disorder or crime
- for the protection of health or morals
- for the protection of the reputation or rights of others
- for preventing the disclosure of information received in confidence
- for maintaining the authority and impartiality of the judiciary.

The contentious nature of these offences demonstrates that it is imperative that policing decisions are made without fear or favour, and that they take into account all of the considerations of the ECHR and Human Rights Act 1998.

13.1 Incitement to racial hatred

Section 18 of the Public Order Act 1986 makes it an offence for a person to use threatening, abusive or insulting words or behaviour, or to display any written material which is threatening, abusive or insulting, intending to stir up racial hatred, or where having regard to all the circumstances racial hatred is likely to be stirred up. An offence under sections 19–22 of the Act includes distribution, broadcasting, performance, public display and possession of inflammatory material.

The Act defines racial hatred as hatred against a group of persons defined by reference to colour, race, nationality (including citizenship) or ethnic or national origins.

An offence under this section may be committed in a public or a private place, except that no offence is committed where the words or behaviour are used, or the written material is displayed, by a person inside a dwelling and are not heard or seen except by other persons in that or another dwelling.

Full details of the Act can be found at the <u>Office of Public Sector Information</u> website.

13.2 Incitement to hatred on the grounds of religion

Section 29B of the Public Order Act 1986 makes it an offence for a person to use threatening words or behaviour, or display any written material which is threatening, with the intention to stir up religious hatred. Sections 29C to 29F of the Act include the offences of distribution, broadcasting, performance, public display and possession of inflammatory material.

Religious hatred means hatred against a group of persons defined by reference to religious belief or lack of religious belief.

An offence under this section may be committed in a public or a private place, except that no offence is committed where the words or behaviour are used, or the written material is displayed, by a person inside a dwelling and are not heard or seen except by other persons in that or another dwelling.

The Act includes section 29J which is designed to protect freedom of expression. This states:

> ...nothing in this Part shall be read or given effect in a way which prohibits or restricts discussion, criticism or expressions of antipathy, dislike, ridicule, insult or abuse of particular religions or the beliefs or practices of their adherents, or of any other belief system or the beliefs or practices of its adherents, or proselytising or urging adherents of a different religion or belief system to cease practicing their religion or belief system.

Full details of the Act can be found at the <u>Office of Public Sector Information</u> website.

13.3 Incitement to hatred based on sexual orientation

Section 29B of the Public Order Act 1986 (as inserted by the Criminal Justice and Immigration Act 2008) makes it an offence for a person to use threatening words or behaviour, or display any written material which is threatening, with the intention to stir up hatred against a group of people defined on the grounds of their sexual orientation. Sections 29C to 29F of the Act include the offences of distribution, broadcasting, performance, public display and possession of inflammatory material.

Hatred on the grounds of sexual orientation means hatred against a group of persons defined by reference to sexual orientation (whether towards persons of the same sex, the opposite sex or both). See section 29AB of the Act.

An offence under this section may be committed in a public or a private place, except that no offence is committed where the words or behaviour are used, or the written material is displayed, by a person inside a dwelling and are not heard or seen except by other persons in that or another dwelling.

The Act includes section 29JA, which is designed to protect freedom of expression. This states:

> In this Part, for the avoidance of doubt, the discussion or criticism of sexual conduct or practices or the urging of persons to refrain from or modify such conduct or practices shall not be taken of itself to be threatening or intended to stir up hatred.

Full details of the Act can be found at the <u>Office of Public Sector Information</u> website.

13.4 Guidance on incitement to hatred offences

The three incitement to hatred offences are not identical. They were created at different times and had different transitions through

Parliament, meaning that each should be considered separately. The most significant difference is that the race offence covers threatening, abusive or insulting words, behaviour or material, whereas the religious and sexual orientation offences cover only threatening words, behaviour or material.

All three offences are committed where the offender intended to stir up hatred. The race offence also includes circumstances where such hatred is likely to be stirred up.

13.5 Action in response to allegations of incitement to hatred

It is essential, if the trust and confidence in the police is to be maintained, that any action in response to these offences is taken without fear or favour. They can cause significant damage and any complaints need to be fully investigated, but the rights of the accused individual also need to be taken into account.

A religious or any other personal belief is no defence to these offences, but the free expression or debate of personal views is a protected human right, which is why the threshold for this offence is set so high. Freedom of expression is a right under Article 10 of the ECHR and Schedule 1 of the Human Rights Act 1998. Full details of the Act can be found at the Office of Public Sector Information website.

REFERENCES

Allen, G. and Langford, D. (2008) *Effective interviewing in social work and social care: A practical guide*, Basingstoke: Palgrave Macmillan.

Asquith, N. (2010) 'Verbal and textual hostility in context', in N. Chakraborti (ed) *Hate crime: Concepts, policy, future directions*, Cullompton: Willan Publishing.

Awan, I. (2014) 'Islamophobia and Twitter: a typology of online hate against Muslims on social media', *Policy & Internet*, 6(2): 133–50.

Awan, I. and Zempi, I. (2016) 'The affinity between online and offline anti-Muslim hate crime: dynamics and impacts', *Aggression and Violent Behaviour*, 27: 1–8.

BBC News (2016) 'Met Police deputy chief links Brexit vote to hate crime rise', 20 July. Available at: http://www.bbc.co.uk/news/uk-england-london-36835966

Bowling, B. and Phillips, C. (2003) 'Racist victimisation in England and Wales', in D.F. Hawkins (ed) *Violent crime: Assessing race and ethnic differences*, Cambridge: Cambridge University Press, pp 154–70.

Caplan, G. (1964) *Principles of preventative psychiatry*, New York: Basic Books.

CERD (Committee on the Elimination of Racial Discrimination) (2016) 'Concluding observations on the twenty-first to twenty-third periodic reports of United Kingdom of Great Britain and Northern Ireland', CERD/c/GBR/Co/21-23. Available at: http://tbinternet.ohchr.org/Treaties/CERD/Shared%20Documents/GBR/CERD_C_GBR_CO_21-23_24985_E.pdf

Chahal, K (1992) *Hidden from view: A study of racial harassment in Preston*, Preston: Preston Borough Council.

Chahal, K. (2003) *Racist harassment support projects: Their role, impact and potential*, York: Joseph Rowntree Foundation.

Chahal, K. (2008) 'Empowerment, "Racist incidents and casework practice"', *Housing, Care and Support*, 11(2): 22–9.

Chahal, K. and Julienne, L. (1999) *'We can't all be white!' Racist victimisation in the UK*, York: Joseph Rowntree Foundation.

Chakraborti, N. and Garland, J. (eds) (2004) *Rural racism*, Cullompton: Willan Publishing.

Chakraborti, N. and Garland, J. (2009) *Hate crime: Impact, causes and responses*, London: Sage Publications Ltd.

Chakraborti, N. (ed) (2010) *Hate crime: Concepts, policy, future directions*, Cullompton, Willan Publishing.

Chakraborti, N. and Hardy, S. (2016) *Healing the harms: Identifying how best to support hate crime victims*, Leicester: University of Leicester.

Chakraborti, N., Garland, J. and Hardy, S. (2014) *The Leicester Hate Crime Project: Findings and conclusions*, Leicester: University of Leicester.

Christie, N. (1986) 'The ideal victim', in E.A. Fattah (ed) *From crime policy to victim policy: Reorienting the justice system*, Basingstoke: Palgrave, pp 17–30.

Christmann, K. and Wong, K. (2010) 'Hate crime victims and hate crime reporting: some impertinent questions' in N. Chakraborti (ed) *Hate crime: Concepts, policy, future directions*, Cullompton: Willan Publishing.

Citron, D.K. (2014) *Hate crimes in cyberspace*, Cambridge, MA : Harvard University Press.

Citron, D. and Norton, H. (2011) 'Intermediaries and hate speech: fostering digital citizenship for our information age', *Boston University Law Review*, 91(4): 1435–84.

College of Policing (2014) *Hate crime operational guidance*, Coventry: College of Policing Limited. Available at: http://library.college. police.uk/docs/college-of-policing/Hate-Crime-Operational-Guidance.pdf

Commission for Racial Equality (2000) *Tackling racial harassment in Scotland: A caseworker's handbook*, London: Commission for Racial Equality.

Corcoran, H., Lader, D. and Smith, K. (2015) 'Hate crime, England and Wales 2014/15'. Available at: https://www.gov.uk/government/uploads/system/uploads/attachment_data/file/467366/hosb0515.pdf

Corcoran, H. and Smith, K. (2016) 'Hate crime, England and Wales, 2015/16'. Available at: https://www.gov.uk/government/uploads/system/uploads/attachment_data/file/559319/hate-crime-1516-hosb1116.pdf

Coulshed, V. and Orme, J. (2006) *Social work practice: An introduction* (4th edn), Basingstoke: Macmillan/BASW.

CPS (Crown Prosecution Service) (2016) *Hate crime report 2014/15 and 2015/16.* Available at: https://www.cps.gov.uk/publications/docs/cps_hate_crime_report_2016.pdf

CPS (Crown Prosecution Service) (no date) 'Victim Personal Statements'. Available at: http://www.cps.gov.uk/legal/v_to_z/victim_personal_statements/

Craig-Henderson, K. and Sloan, L.R. (2003) 'After the hate: helping psychologists help victims of racist hate crime', *Clinical Psychology: Science and Practice*, 10(4): 481–90.

Crown Office and Procurator Fiscal Office (2016) 'Hate crime in Scotland 2015–16'. Available at: http://www.crownoffice.gov.uk/images/Documents/Equality_Diversity/Hate%20Crime%20in%20Scotland%202015-16.pdf

Curry-Stevens, A. (2011) 'Persuasion: infusing advocacy practice with insights from anti-oppression practice', *Journal of Social Work*, 12(4): 345–63.

Daniels, J. (2013) 'Race and racism in Internet studies: a review and critique', *New Media & Society*, 15(5): 695–719.

Day, E. (2013) 'Mary Beard: "I almost didn't feel such generic, violent misogyny was about me"', *The Observer*, 26 January. Available at https://www.theguardian.com/books/2013/jan/26/mary-beard-question-time-internet-trolls

Dhooper, S.S. and Moore, E.S. (2000) *Social work practice with culturally diverse people*, Thousand Oaks, CA: Sage Publications.

Dick, S. (2008) *Homophobic hate crime: The Gay British Crime Survey*, London: Stonewall.

Dignan, J. (2005) *Understanding victims and restorative justice*, Maidenhead: Open University Press.

Dixon, T. and O'Hara, M. (no date) 'Communication skills'. Available at http://cw.routledge.com/textbooks/9780415537902/data/learning/11_Communication%20Skills.pdf

Egan, G. (2014) *The skilled helper: A problem-management and opportunity-development approach to helping*, Pacific Grove, CA: Brooks/Cole.

EHRC (Equality and Human Rights Commission) (2011) *Hidden in plain sight: Inquiry into disability-related harassment*, Manchester: EHRC.

Ellin, J. (2003) *Listening helpfully: How to develop your counselling skills*, London: Souvenir Press.

European Commission (2012) 'Establishing minimum standards on the rights, support and protection of victims of crime, and replacing Council Framework Decision 2001/220/JHA, Directive 2012/29/EU of the European Parliament and of the Council'. Available at: http://eur-lex.europa.eu/legal-content/EN/TXT/PDF/?uri=CELEX:32012L0029&from=EN

European Commission (2016) 'Code of conduct on countering illegal hate speech online'. Available at: http://ec.europa.eu/justice/fundamental-rights/files/hate_speech_code_of_conduct_en.pdf (accessed 27 August 2016).

European Forum for Victim Services (no date) 'The social rights of victims of crime', Victim Support Europe.

Everly, G.S. (2001) 'Thoughts on early intervention', *International Journal of Emergency Mental Health*, 3(4): 207–10.

Fook, J. (2016) *Social work: A critical approach to practice*, London: Sage.

FRA (European Union Agency for Fundamental Rights) (2014) *Victims of crime in the EU: The extent and nature of support for victims*, Vienna: European Union Agency for Fundamental Rights.

FRA (2016) *Ensuring justice for hate crime victims: Professional perspectives*, Vienna: European Union Agency for Fundamental Rights.

Garland, J. (2010) 'The victimisation of goths and the boundaries of hate crime', in N. Chakraborti (ed) *Hate crime: Concepts, policy, future directions*, Cullompton: Willan Publishing.

Garland, J. and Chakraborti, N. (2012) 'Divided by a common concept? Assessing the implications of different conceptualisations of hate crime in the European Union', *European Journal of Criminology*, 9(1): 38–51.

Gibbs, G. (1988) *Learning by doing: A guide to teaching and learning methods*, London: Further Education Unit.

Goodey, J. (2011) '"Race", religion and victimisation: UK and European response', in S. Walklate (ed) *Handbook of victims and victimology*, Abingdon: Routledge.

Goodman, D. (2001) *Promoting diversity and social justice: Educating people from privileged groups*, Thousand Oaks, CA: Sage.

Guasp, A., Gammon, A. and Ellison, G (2013) *Homophobic hate crime: The Gay British Crime Survey 2013*, London: Stonewall.

Harms, L. (2007) *Working with people: Communication skills for reflective practice*, Melbourne: Oxford University Press.

Hasebrink, U., Livingstone, S., Haddon, L. and Olafsson, K. (2009) *Comparing children's online opportunities and risks across Europe: Cross-national comparisons for EU Kids Online*, EU Kids Online project report, London: LSE.

Hawkins, D. F. (2003) *Violent crime: Assessing race and ethnic differences*, Cambridge: Cambridge University Press.

Healy, K. (2012) *Social work methods and skills: The essential foundations of practice*, Basingstoke: Palgrave MacMillan.

Hepworth, D.H., Rooney, R.H., Rooney, G.D., Strom-Gottfried, K. and Larsen, J. (2010) *Direct social work practice: Theory and skills*, Belmont, CA: Brooks/Cole CENGAGE Learning.

Herek, G.M., Gillis, J.R., Cogan, J.C. and Glunt, E.K. (1997) 'Hate crime victimisation among lesbian, gay and bisexual adults', *Journal of Interpersonal Violence*, 12(2): 195–215.

Herman, J.L. (2005) 'Justice from the victim's perspective', *Violence Against Women*, 11(5): 571–602.

Hodkinson, M. (2008) 'United in the name of tolerance', *The Observer*, 2 August. Available at: https://www.theguardian.com/uk/2008/aug/03/ukcrime.sophielancaster

Home Office (2016) *Action against hate: The UK government's plan for tackling hate crime*, London: Home Office.

Iganski, P. (2001) 'Hate crimes hurt more', *American Behavioral Scientist*, 45(4): 626–38.

Iganski, P. (2008) '*Hate crime' and the city*, Bristol: The Policy Press.

Iganski, P. and Lagou, S. (2015) 'Hate crimes hurt some more than others: implications for the just sentencing of offenders', *Journal of Interpersonal Violence*, 30(10): 1696–718.

Iganski, P. and Levin, J. (2015) *Hate crime: A global perspective*, New York, NY: Routledge.

Jacks, W. and Adler, J.R. (2015) 'A proposed typology of online hate crime', *Open Access Journal of Forensic Psychology*, 7: 64–89. Available at: http://eprints.mdx.ac.uk/18930/

Jalota, S. (2004) 'Supporting victims of rural racism: learning lessons from a dedicated racial harassment project', in N. Chakraborti and J. Garland (eds) *Rural racism*, Cullompton: Willan Publishing.

Kees, S., Iganski, P., Kusch, R., Swider, M. and Chahal, K. (2016) *Hate crime victim support in Europe: A practical guide*, Dresden: RAA Sachsen E.V.

Koprowska, J. (2014) *Communication and interpersonal skills in social work*, London: Sage.

Lemos&Crane (2004a) *Interviewing victims and witnesses: Guide for housing practitioners (part one)*, London: Lemos&Crane.

Lemos&Crane (2004b) *Interviewing victims and witnesses: Guide (part two)*, London: Lemos&Crane.

Levin, B. (1999) 'Hate crimes: worse by definition', *Journal of Contemporary Criminal Justice*, 15(1): 6–21.

Lishman, J. (1994) *Communication in social work*, Basingstoke: Macmillan/BASW.

Lishman, J. (2009) *Communication in social work* (2nd edn), Basingstoke: Palgrave Macmillan.

Macpherson, W. (1999) *The Stephen Lawrence inquiry*, London: HMSO.

Maslach, C., Jackson, S. and Leiter, M. (1996) *Maslach burnout inventory manual*, Palo Alto, CA: Consulting Psychologists Press.

May-Chahal, C., Mason, C., Rashid, A., Walkerdine, J., Rayson, P. and Greenwood, P. (2014) 'Safeguarding cyborg childhoods: incorporating the on/offline behaviour of children into everyday social work practices', *British Journal of Social Work*, 44(3): 596–614.

Mayer, J.E. and Timms, N. (1970) *The client speaks: Working class impressions of casework*, London: Routledge and Kegan Paul.

McDonald, M. (2012) *Know your rights on the Victims' Directive*, Dublin: Irish Council for Civil Liberties.

Mehrabian, A. (1972) *Non-verbal communication*, Chicago, IL: Aldine-Atherton.

Ministry of Justice (2015) 'Code of practice for victims of crime'. Available at: https://www.gov.uk/moj

Neville, L. (2009) *Interpersonal skills for the people professions: Learning from practice*, Exeter: Reflect Press.

Newham Monitoring Project (2000) *Twentieth anniversary annual report 1999–2000*, London: Newham Monitoring Project.

ODIHR (Office for Democratic Institutions and Human Rights) (2009) *Preventing and responding to hate crimes: A resource guide for NGOs in the OSCE region*, Warsaw: OSCE Office for Democratic Institutions and Human Rights.

Ofcom (Office of Communications) (2015) *Children and parents: Media use and attitudes report*, London: Ofcom.

ONS (Office for National Statistics) (2016) *Internet access – households and individuals: 2016*, London: ONS.

Pattoni, L. (2012) *Strengths-based approaches for working with individuals*, Glasgow: IRISS.

Payne, M. (1998) *Modern social work theory*, Basingstoke: Palgrave.

Places for People (2015) 'Community safety: a summary of our "Statement of community safety policy and procedure"'. Available at: http://www.placesforpeople.co.uk/media/190913/community_safety_policy_statement_mar_2015.pdf

Police Service of Northern Ireland (2016) 'Statistical press notice: The PSNI's statistical reports: 1st April 2015 - 31st March 2016'. Available at: https://www.psni.police.uk/globalassets/news-and-appeals/latest-news/news-stories/2016/may/120516-psni-crime-stats/psni-statistical-press-release-2015_16-final-for-web.pdf

PostRefRacism (2016) 'Post-referendum racism and xenophobia: the role of social media activism in challenging the normalisation of xeno-racist narratives'. Available at: http://www.irr.org.uk/news/post-referendum-racism-and-the-importance-of-social-activism/

Robinson, L. (1998) *Race, communication and the caring professions*, Buckingham: Open University Press.

Rogers, C.R. (1957) 'The necessary and sufficient conditions of therapeutic personality change', *Journal of Consulting Psychology*, 21: 95–103.

Rogers, C.R. (1980) *A way of being*, Boston, MA: Houghton Mifflin.

Schon, D. (1983) *The reflective practitioner: How professionals think in action*, New York, NY: Basic Books.

Schweppe, J. (2013) 'The EU directive on victims of crime'. Available at: http://www.internationalhatestudies.com/the-eu-directive-on-victims-of-crime/ (accessed 12 August 2016).

Seden, J. (2000) *Counselling skills in social work practice*, Buckingham: Open University Press.

Shebib, B. (2003) *Choices: Counseling skills for social workers and other professionals*, Boston, Allyn and Bacon.

Silva, L., Mondal, M., Correa, D., Benevenuto, F. and Weber, I. (2016) 'Analyzing the targets of hate in online social media', Cornell University Library. Available at: http://arxiv.org/pdf/1603.07709v1.pdf

Smale, G., Tuson, G. and Statham, D. (2000) *Social work and social problems: Working towards social inclusion and social change*, London: Macmillan Press.

Suler, J. (2004) 'Online disinhibition effect', *CyberPsychology and Behavior*, 7: 321–6.

Tell MAMA (2014) 'Facebook report: Rotherham, hate, and the far-right online'. Available at: http://tellmamauk.org/wp-content/uploads/2014/09/Rotherham.pdf

Thompson, N. (2003) *Communication and language: A handbook of theory and practice*, Basingstoke: Palgrave Macmillan.

Thompson, N. (2011a) *Promoting equality: Working with diversity and difference*, Basingstoke: Palgrave Macmillan.

Thompson, N. (2011b) *Crisis intervention*, Lyme Regis: Russell House.

Trevithick, P. (2000) *Social work skills: A practice handbook*, Buckingham: Open University Press.

Trevithick, P. (2012) *Social work skills and knowledge: A practice handbook*, Maidenhead: Open University Press.

Van Boven, T. (2013) 'Victim-orientated perspectives: rights and realities', in T. Bonacker and C. Safferling (eds) *Victims of international crimes: An interdisciplinary discourse*, The Hague: Asser Press.

Victim Support (2006) *Crime and prejudice: The support needs of victims of hate crime*, London: Victim Support.

Victim Support Europe (2013) 'Handbook for implementation of legislation and best practice for victims of crime in Europe.' Available at http://victimsupporteurope.eu/activeapp/wp-content/files_mf/1385974688NewVersionVSEHandbookforImplementation.pdf

Victim Support Europe (no date) 'Victim Support Europe manifesto 2014–19'. Available at: http://victimsupporteurope.eu/activeapp/wp-content/files_mf/1382343287FinalDesignedVSEManifesto20142019.pdf

Virdee, S. (1995) *Racial violence and harassment*, London: Policy Studies Institute.

Walter, M. and Hoyle, C (2010) 'Healing harms and engendering tolerance; the promise of restorative justice for hate crime' in N. Chakraborti (ed) *Hate crime: Concepts, policy and future directions*, Cullompton: Willan Publishing.

Williams, M. and Tregidga, J. (2014) 'Hate crime victimization in Wales: psychological and physical impacts across seven hate crime victim types', *British Journal of Criminology*, 54: 946–67.

Winterdyk, J. and Antonopoulos, G. (eds) (2008) *Racist victimization: International reflections and perspectives*, Aldershot: Ashgate.

Zempi, I. and Awan, I. (2016) *Islamophobia: Lived experiences of online and offline victimisation*, Bristol: The Policy Press.

Zimbardo, P.G. (1969) 'The human choice: individuation, reason, and order vs. deindividuation, impulse, and chaos', in W.J. Arnold and D. Levine (eds) *Nebraska symposium on motivation*, Lincoln, NE: University of Nebraska Press.

Index

Page numbers in *italics* refer to tables.

Lightning Source UK Ltd.
Milton Keynes UK
UKHW021846060422
401197UK00005B/180